Instructor's Manual to Accompany

A Collection of Cases in Marketing Management

Second Edition

H. Robert Dodge
Youngstown State University

William G. Zikmund
Oklahoma State University

West Publishing Company
St. Paul   New York   Los Angeles   San Francisco

COPYRIGHT © 1987 by WEST PUBLISHING CO.
50 West Kellogg Boulevard
P.O. Box 64526
St. Paul, MN 55164-1003

ISBN 0-314-34765-8

TABLE OF CONTENTS

CONTROL OF MARKETING ACTIVITIES

NOT-FOR-PROFIT MARKETING

TSR HOBBIES, INC. -- "DUNGEONS AND DRAGONS"[1]

CASE OBJECTIVES

1. To better understand the fundamentals of target marketing and market segmentation.

2. To illustrate how marketing strategy must change over the course of a product life cycle.

3. To illustrate a channel conflict problem.

SUMMARY

This case describes a small company that made a big splash in the specialized hobby market. Upper management's intimate understanding of the product and hobby enthusiasts contributed to TSR's tremendous initial success. However, entry into the mass market resulted in serious problems for an inexperienced management team.

TSR began by marketing a complex game to experienced game players. As the product matured, younger groups became interested in the game and TSR changed its market segmentation strategy and expanded its product line. As the company increasingly aimed toward the mass market, it expanded its promotional efforts and distribution channels.

TSR's product line included games like "Top Secret", "Boot Hill", "Gamma World", "Star Frontiers", and "Dungeons and Dragons." Their most popular game, "Dungeons and Dragons" was first introduced in 1974. 1000 sets were sold in the first year. Within eight years, they were selling nearly 750,000 games per year. This growth, however, was not reflective of the skill level of the company's top management. Problems such as personnel turnover and employee dissatisfaction plagued the company.

TSR's main competitors were game giants such as Mattel, Parker Brothers, Milton Bradley, and Ideal. These giants provided stiff competition in the game market. This stiff competition and internal turmoil created many problems for TSR. These problems are best understood by focusing discussion on the following topics.

QUESTIONS

1. What are the differences between mass marketing and marketing to specialized hobby shops?

2. What were the market segmentation and target marketing strategy

---

[1] This teaching note is based on materials prepared by Margaret L. Friedman, University of Wisconsin.

considerations?

3. What were the pluses and, more importantly the minuses of rapid growth?

CASE ANALYSIS

1. The differences between mass marketing and marketing to specified hobby shops.

The overriding difference is the fierce competition in the mass market that TSR was insulated from in the hobby market. Whether TSR should have tackled the mass market is a topic worthy of discussion. TSR was clearly not ready to compete against the large and well-entrenched toy and hobby giants.

The mass market environment also differs from the hobby market in other important ways in addition to the examples given in the case, e.g., the characteristics of demand and payment practices. First, the life cycles of products in the mass market are, typically, relatively short. This implies a major and ongoing commitment to investment in new product development. Secondly, the specialized kind of assistance provided for consumers in the hobby market is not provided by sales clerks in the mass market. The product was sold in hobby shops and had to sell itself in the mass market. Given the product's esoteric nature, this is an important limitation. Finally, TSR's distribution system was not designed to take up the slack in the mass market and provide special services to retailers to push the product through the channel. TSR was not prepared to supply mass retailers with aids such as point-of-purchase displays or window banners that are important in mass merchandising but not so important in the specialized hobby market.

When TSR entered the mass market, it inadvertently turned its back on loyal hobby shop owners, the retailers who were responsible for TSR's meteoric rise. Hobby retailers were alienated since all they had traditionally expected and received from TSR was prompt delivery of orders. Now they were not even able to get the product because of the chronic out-of-stock conditions at headquarters. TSR had overcommitted itself with its rapid entry into the mass market. Furthermore, when it closed its own retail hobby shop to solve a channel conflict problem, it may have sent a negative message to some hobby shops concerning level of commitment to that market.

2. Market segmentation and target marketing strategy considerations.

Initially, with no marketing effort, the product was sold directly to target consumers, experienced gamers with a passion for complex, role playing/fantasy games. Over time as the product became known in other circles, TSR segmented their growing market on the basis of a combination of demographics, psychographics, and buyer behavior. The target market included older male teens who were described as introverted, intellectual, and eccentric and were willing to shop around for the "Dungeons and Dragons" product. The product was distributed through hobby shops at that time. This exclusive distribution arrangement gave the product an aura of elitism and mystique.

As the product became more generally known, mainly through word-of-mouth advertising, TSR made the strategic decision to take "Dungeons and Dragons" products to the mass market. TSR never intended to forsake their loyal hobby market, but were simply implementing a differentiated target marketing strategy. It expanded its product mix to include products targeted to younger males, females, and the mass market of game players. The results of implementing such an expansion strategy were that 1) TSR simply did not have the marketing clout to compete successfully in the crowded mass market of entrenched competitors, 2) TSR slighted its loyal specialty customer base, and 3) TSR diluted its image and created customer confusion.

Issues of segmentation and targeting always beg the question: "What share of what market do we want and are able to serve?" Having carved out a lucrative niche for itself, TSR failed to take realistic stock of its resources. TSR had become a specialist in a small but very profitable market. Assuming that its specialized talent would automatically transfer to the mass market without careful planning and seasoned management was the fatal flaw in TSR's logic. A phenomenal rate of growth had put TSR in a reactive, not proactive mode of operation.

The problem can also be couched in terms of product life cycle analysis. Is the PLC to be expected from "Dungeons and Dragons" products comparable to a "Monopoly" or "Scrabble" which exhibit traditional cycles with desirably long maturity stages, or is it more akin to a fad, exhibiting an abbreviated PLC? Assuming that the latter is probably the case, the commitment of resources to expand the target market for the product is a reasonable strategy to consider to prolong the life of the product. Still, serving the hobby enthusiasts with a variety of products and foregoing the mass market may have been a profitable strategy in the long run. Further, one has to question how objective TSR was in assessing its ability to serve the lucrative mass market.

Finally, TSR's goal of doubling sales every year must be questioned. Such an absolute goal, while desirably quantitative, is not placed in a hierarchical context with other goals, is questionable with respect to realism and must be criticized in terms of consistency, not with other goals, but with available resources and talent.

3. <u>The pluses and, more importantly, the minuses of rapid growth</u>.

This case provides an excellent opportunity to discuss the dark side of growth and expansion, i.e., the tremendous amount of financial marketing and management resources it requires. So much emphasis is placed upon the value of growth (and market share) in marketing management texts that it might be considered by students as an important goal to achieve at all costs. Much less attention is given to the problems with growth, particularly for small firms with inexperienced management.

Uncontrolled growth can result in many problems, several of which are illustrated in this case:

1) a volatile organizational chart, causing operating efficiencies,
2) problems with employee morale and turnover, due to mismanagement and nepotism,
3) lack of expertise to lead a company suddenly thrust into competition with much larger organizations, and
4) damage to current product image and position.

The tremendous rate of growth required an inflow of personnel, disrupting organizational charts and established roles and chains of command, as well as the smooth running of daily operations. For example, 90,000 copies of the board for a new fantasy foresty game had to be sent back to the printer because they had been folded the wrong way and would not fit in the box. A similar mishap was mentioned in the case where two different games were packaged in boxes with identical graphics on the box top. The tendency of top menagement to want to "share the wealth" and cater to friends and relatives as a primary hiring motive and, in one case, rationale for expansion, not only created ill-will among employees, but also resulted in a decision that drained company resources. Perhaps the nepotism was seen as a risk-reducing strategy by management, but it is generally bad practice. TSR's inability to service their established customers well while they expanded their markets is yet another indication that it was a matter of too much growth too fast. At one point, a computer system did not show when TSR was out of a product, one that customers were "screaming" for. Finally, the mysterious and elitist nature of the original product, attributes that made it such a success, were at odds with entry into the mass market. As Coors beer lost some of its appeal when its distribution was extended to regions of the country east of the Rockies, so too did "Dungeons and Dragons" lose some of its appeal when it was no longer for a "select few" but for the masses.

One gets the impression from the facts of this case that the uncontrolled growth of this company is unhealthy to its future and that current management is perhaps not capable of controlling the company and directing it wisely. When the company was young and small, employees reminisce that on a Thursday afternoon one might come up with a new product idea, and by Monday it would be ready for market. The organizational climate reflected the attitude, "if you have a good idea, go with it!". As the organization chart grew more complex and larger, a more disciplined management approach was needed. An important question is whether TSR management is capable of making such a transition in style and execution. If current management recognizes the need for expertise, and is willing to relinquish some authority, perhaps the firm could hire more experienced managers to aid in running the company. Imported, experienced managers would introduce such practices as the pacing of growth, more strategic planning and orderly implementation of plans, improved control systems, and management and employee training to tame the runaway growth. The founders of TSR would forsake automony for long fun viability, which others have been willing to do when thrust into keen competition with major league competitors (i.e., Steven Jobs, Apple Inc.).

On the other hand the trmendous growth TSR enjoyed is a great success story despite the recent turmoil. TSR created a new segment in the game industry and became a strong leader in that segment. As of the end of

November 1983, "Management remains convinced that TSR will come out of the turmoil all the stronger. Mr. Blume indicated that continuing operations were profitable last year, despite the fact that the write-off of the needlework company resulted in a loss. He jauntily says that there are many prospective suitors, but that TSR won't sell" (<u>Wall Street Journal</u>, November 25, 1983).

ST. PETER'S HOSPITAL[1]

CASE OBJECTIVES

The St. Peter's Hospital case provides students with an opportunity to supply several textbook concepts to a new health service. The case was originally prepared as an in-class exercise for a group of assistant hospital administrators enrolled in a one-day seminar on marketing and health care. The case contains sufficient data on the marketing mix to allow beginning marketing students to see how these variables must work together. Some data were intentionally omitted because the primary objective of the case is to encourage students to apply concepts rather than analyze data.

SUMMARY

The new administration of a 200 bed hospital is considering a number of areas to develop. Among these areas is the possible creation of a hospice program. The hospital's Board enthusiastically endorsed the idea and quickly they supported a team to study the feasibility of a hospice program. After three months of study, the team reported its findings at a board meeting. Several different opinions were put forth during the meeting: four members wanted to get more information; one wanted to postpone the hospice program to work on other priority areas; and six members wanted to proceed with the development of the hospice. Finally, the Board decided to retain a consultant. The primary functions of the consultants were to: (1) make a recommendation regarding the feasibility of the hospice program; and (2) develop a complete marketing plan for the proposed hospice. To help the consultant, the Board provided an outline of specific marketing-related areas to be covered and a series of four exhibits summarizing all the data they had relevant to promotion, distribution, pricing and service offering.

QUESTIONS

1. Given John Rowe's seven priority areas, is it appropriate for the board of Directors to identify the development of a hospice as its number one priority? Explain.

2. Discuss the rationale used by the board in concluding that a hospice should be developed. Support or refute the rationale.

3. Do the four topic areas to be covered in the marketing consultant's study include all the basics of a good marketing study? Should other areas be included? If so, what?

4. How should Exhibits 2 through 4 be utilized by the consultants? What

---

[1]. This teaching note is based on materials prepared by Charles H. Patti and Debra Low, from Cases in Advertising and Promotion Management (New York: John Wiley & Sons; 1983).

other information might be useful in making marketing decisions?

5. Are the marketing questions raised by the board valid? Should other topics be covered? If so, what?

6. Demonstrate how the "four P's" of marketing can be integrated in this situation.

CASE ANALYSIS

1. Given John Rowe's seven priority areas, is it appropriate for the Board of Directors to identify the development of a hospice as its number one priority? Explain.

   Yes, it is appropriate for the board to identify hospice as its top priority because it is ultimately the board's responsibility to define the broad directions and priorities for the hospital rather than the chief executive's.

2. Discuss the rationale used by the board in concluding that a hospice should be developed. Support or refute the rationale.

   The rationale used by the board is unclear. One board member, an oncologist, briefly explained the concept. Another board member, a nun, believed that the hospice concept would be congruent with the mission of a Catholic hospital. No consideration appears to have been given to demand, need, economic feasibility, service (product) mix, quality of care, type of hospice program, and other "hard" data.

3. Do the four topic areas to be covered in the marketing consultant's study include all the basics of a good marketing study? Should other areas be included? If so, what?

   The plan includes some of the basics but not all. The plan could also include a more complete analysis of the "consumer" (e.g. physicians' perceptions of the hospice concept as they refer their patients), the market (e.g. the competitive environment in terms of other hospitals' service development, pricing, distribution of services and promotional strategies), and an analysis of industry trends.

4. How should Exhibits 2 through 4 be utilized by the consultant? What other information might be useful in making marketing decisions?

   The four exhibits should be used as a source of information but should be supplemented with additional data. The additional data should include local market data, local consumer data (e.g. physicians' attitudes, health care consumers' attitudes) and local health industry data.

5. Are the marketing questions raised by the board valid? Should other topics be covered? If so, what?

    The marketing questions raised are valid. Other questions to be considered should include:

    A. Can the hospital afford to make a long-term commitment to hospice, even if it is not profit-generating?

    B. Will the hospice utilize existing staff expertise or require additional personnel?

    C. Is there a demand for hospice services by physicians? patients?

    D. Does the hospice concept fit into St. Peter's services mix?

6. Demonstrate how the "four P's" of marketing can be integrated in this situation.

    The four P's incorporate product, place, price, and promotion.

    The consultant's marketing plan will encompass an analysis of the hospice as a "product" or service and will more specifically look at the most appropriate "product" criteria to incorporate in the hospice program that he proposes.

    In terms of "place," the consultant will consider the various distribution attributes of the alternative hospice models and will additionally evaluate other distribution strategies that can be built into the service concept.

    For "price," the consultant will consider costs to provide hospice services and ancillary services, costs of labor, costs of overhead and will determine the most feasible fee schedules based on what the market will bear and on what insurance companies, Medicare and Medicaid will cover.

    For "promotion," the consultant will evaluate various communications approaches that may be taken, following the development of measurable promotional objectives.

POTTY POSIES[1]

CASE OBJECTIVES

This case illustrates the product development process as it occurs in a smaller firm, and is an interesting contrast to the New England Mop Company's approach with the typical process taken by large firms. The case also provides a useful vehicle for discussing the interrelationships between product, promotion, price, and channel-of-distribution decisions. It allows the student to get an early look at the variables that can be influenced by the marketing manager. It also allows the student to participate in the development and evaluation of a product-market plan. The case can also be used to explore the effects of environmental variables (competition, demand, etc.) on the firm's marketing efforts.

SUMMARY

New England Mop Company, Inc. is a 28-year-old small manufacturer of wool mops.

The New England Mop Company is considering expanding into the distribution of toilet bowl deodorizers. The only justification given for the choice of this new product was that it fit new England Mop's channel of distribution.

The deodorizer will be made of colored cakes of paradichlorobenzene molded in the shapes of flowers. Although the concept of a colored bowl deodorizer has been attempted before by other manufacturers, there is not a similar product on the market at the present time.

The president and owner, Mr. Ronald Felici, must decide on the feasibility of marketing the new product to be known as "Potty Posies." The product is a colored paradichlorobenzene cake with a flower shape and scent, which is to be hung in toilet bowls as a deodorizer. The new product would be distributed through a portion of their channels of distribution, notably supermarkets and mass merchandisers. A product mock-up has been shown at a large trade show where buyer enthusiasm was very strong. However, there are still some unanswered questions such as the size of the market and the sales potential for the product. Mr. Felici wonders whether the product should be marketed immediately, more information gathered, or the idea abandoned because of this uncertainty.

QUESTIONS

1. Evaluate the product development process of New England Mop Co., Inc., for Potty Posies.

---

[1] This teaching note is based upon a teaching note prepared by David Louden, Northeast Lousiana University

2. What would you have done differently? Keep in mind New England Mop is a fairly small company.

3. How large is the market? What additional information is needed or desired if potty posies is to be marketed?

4. Are the product design and name appropriate?

5. What price do you recommend and why?

6. What channel of distribution do you recommend?

7. How should Potty Posies be promoted?

CASE ANALYSIS

1. Evaluate the product development process of New England Mop Co., Inc., for Potty Posies.

    The product development process typically includes the stages of idea generation, screening, business analysis, product market testing, and commercialization. Discussion may center on how each of these stages differs for the small company as compared to the large firm. For example, the small firm generates fewer new product ideas, its sources are likely to be outside the firm, it has a less formal screening mechanism, business analysis is likely to be less rigorous, and little or no product or market testing may be done before commercialization.

2. What would you have done differently? Keep in mind New England Mop is a fairly small company.

    Students are likely to offer many suggestions for improving New England Mop's product development process. Some of these will probably tend toward rather grandiose ideas of things that would really be nice to do, but simply aren't possible for a small, cash-poor firm like this one. Therefore, each suggestion should be assessed in this light.

3. Is there a market for Potty Posies? What additional information is needed or desired?

    The overall paradichlorobenzene market is large and amounts to between $10 and $15 million per year. Of this, approximately $5 million is spent on toilet bowl deodorizers annually. If New England Mop could get just 5 percent of this market they would have sales of Potty posies of $250,000. This is over 60 percent of current mop sales. In addition, service merchandisers estimate that toilet bowl deodorizers are the second largest selling item behind panty hose in the non-food sections of supermarkets. Obviously the market is there, the question is whether Potty Posies and New England Mop will be able to grab a significant piece of the action.

Thus there are many unanswered questions faced by the company, the most important of which are the following:

What share of this market can Potty Posies be expected to capture?

Why did colored cakes of this product not succeed before?

Will price be a barrier for this product?

Does the product fit well enough with present channels?

Can an adequate manufacturer be found for this product, especially in the face of petroleum-based chemical shortages?

How much of the enthusiasm at the trade show can be converted into sales to retailers?

Until answers are provided for these questions, the feasibility of marketing the product is uncertain. Additional information would be desirable but is not absolutely necessary.

Students should be asked how they would go about finding the additional information they think is necessary, once again keeping the limitations of a small company uppermost in mind.

4. Are the product and design and name appropriate?

The product appears to be an improvement on present toilet bowl deodorizers. The product is larger, comes in colors, is scented, and is shaped in the form of a flower. The name at first seems too cute and trite for a product of this sort. However, the name is descriptive and unique. Students tend to laugh at the name, then they are usually at a loss when you challenge them to come up with a better name.

5. What price do you recommend and why?

Price is one of the key variables in this case and tends to prompt considerable discussion among the students. Some students note that the proposed price of $.69 for a 5-ounce cake amounts to $1.38 per ounce compared to $.13 per ounce for the standard 3-ounce cakes that sell for $.39. New England Mop is planning to sell a larger size at a higher price per ounce. This is contrary to common practice where larger sizes of household products usually have lower prices per ounce. The question remains whether the unique features of Potty Posies will allow it to be sold at a premium price. After much arguing, most students say the price is adequate for now.

6. What channel of distribution do you recommend?

New England Mop sells through a system of 43 reps who are paid a commission of 6 percent of sales. Although dust mops were traditionally sold through department and hardware stores, the firm had gradually shifted towards larger mass merchandisers and supermarkets. Thus new channels seemed ideally suited to the proposed toilet bowl deodorizer. Since the reps already call on the intended channel members, they will probably not object to taking on the new item. Most students think the reps will welcome the new product.

7. How should Potty Posies be promoted?

There are an endless number of things that could be done to promote Potty Posies, but most of them are too expensive for New England Mop Company. Certainly a large co-op promotional allowance like the $.50 offer on the mops is not reasonable. Toilet bowl deodorizers are rarely advertised and it makes sense to push them with point-of-purchase display racks. This takes advantage of impulse purchases and simplifies restocking in the stores.

Actual Company Decision

As it turned out, New England Mop did introduce the product at $.69 and they called it Potty Posies. In little more than a year and a half they sold $400,000 of the toilet bowl deodorizers. However, the project was not without its problems. Although they started out at $.69, the price was later reduced to $.59, indicating the initial price may have been too high. They also ran into breakage problems with the cakes because of the flower design. The biggest problem was that the manufacturer stopped making Potty Posies for New England Mop because of the bother of having to clean the molds to make cakes in different colors. New England mop was unable to find another supplier and the product was discontinued. New England Mop was not too upset with the loss of Potty Posies because the item had been profitable and they were able to switch to the production of needlepoint kits. These kits could be made with the same wool used in the mops and sales greatly exceeded expectations. As a final comment we might note that other manufacturers of toilet bowl deodorizers copied New England Mop's display stand, added scents to their products, and wrapped their cakes in colored cellophane to cover up their white appearance.

TARGET STORES[1]

CASE OBJECTIVES

To understand the effects on performance of an emphasis upon understanding consumers and serving their needs well.

To understand the importance and effects of written policy statements that can provide guidance to specific marketing decisions.

To understand the need for even the best policies to be adapted over time to changing environments and circumstances.

SUMMARY

Target is one of the premier successes among discount department stores. While K-Mart is larger, K-Mart has experienced difficulties in reaching the white-collar worker to which Target's marketing programs have been directed very effectively. Today, however, K-Mart has become more aggressive and effective. Additionally, Wal-Mart is attacking Target in some markets, drawing on its own base of efficiency and good customer service developed in rural geographic areas. Many other "off-price" merchandisers, such as Marshall's, T.J. Maxx, and Burlington Coat Factory (to mention only a few of the more prominent), are also serious competition. What unique position can Target maintain in such an environment and how can that mission be expressed in a written policy statement?

Results of the study can be presented as background formation for the case.

QUESTIONS

1. Of what value is a written policy statement? How important is a mission statement to managers engaged in strategic marketing?

2. What role does proper execution play in the carrying out of a corporate mission?

3. What environmental changes are likely to affect Target's future?

4. If Target is to grow what changes need to be made in its marketing strategy?

---

[1] Teaching note based on materials prepared by Roger Blackwell, Wayne Talarzyk and James Engle, Contemporary Cases in Consumer Behavior (Hinsdale, Ill: Dryden Press, 1984)

CASE ANALYSIS

1. A written policy statement is of no more value than the vision of management originating the statement and the continuing commitment to carry out the policy. Certainly, the vision and commitment are more important than words on paper. However, the Target management appears to have put on paper the reality that existed in management's commitment.

The content of the Guidelines--both words and management commitment--is outstanding and has been critical to the enormous success of Target relative to other discount department stores. It is apparent that Target has selected the correct market targets for growth in the 1980s, has attempted to distribute merchandise consistent with lifestyles, and has sought and achieved an understanding of what is meant by "value" to these segments and the integrated approach to retailing required to deliver "value".

2. Target has discipline in its execution of the Guidelines. This is reflected in the merchandise stocked, method of display, efficiency of check-out systems, advertisements (clear, informative, national brands, contemporary image with people wearing apparel that is clearly consistent with the lifestyle targets), and atmospherics of the store.

3. The changes in the environment most likely to affect Target in the future include:

    a. the increase in the number and market importance of YUPPIES (young, urban professionals), who may want even more upscale merchandise than is reflected in the Target market definition.
    b. intensive price competition from "off-price merchandisers," who will feature national brands but who typically rely on close-outs, special purchases, minimum service and return policy, and other marketing strategies, putting Target's reliance on national brands in some jeopardy for direct price comparisons.
    c. continuing growth in areas of the United States where Target has little representation (50 percent of all population growth between 1980 and 2000 is expected to occur in three states: Florida, Texas, and California, according to U.S. Census projections).
    d. growth in product categories that require considerable service and labor involvement, frequently served well by specialty stores. Computer products and other high-growth consumer electronics are examples (multi-function telephones, audio discs, large screen and projection television, etc.).
    e. rapid increases in affluence (driven mostly by two-income families) that allow much more personal expression in products.

The Guidelines should reflect the above-mentioned environmental changes and must deal with the dual directions of greater efficiency in operations and more flexibility in service.

4. Target will not undertake a fundamental re-orientation of its strategy but will need strategy extensions if it is to continue its previous rapid growth in the future. This will need to include more services--possibly through in-store videotext presentation or other technical innovations-- and specialty merchandise and service development. New forms of

electronic payment systems, improved logistics performance, and integration of electronic POS systems will be required to maintain the price competitiveness and the Guidelines seek with the quality of merchandise and service also described by the Guidelines. As market segments mature, Target will have to move with them (possibly with better fashion, the addition of financial services, improved service for some departments) or forfeit to other retailers the market that made great advances in the Seventies, falling back on markets of the Eighties that are similar to those in the Seventies but much smaller in numbers (decline of the 20-30s age group in the Eighties compared to huge increases in that group during the Seventies).

TEACHING IDEAS

Students can be encouraged to make comparisons between the major discount stores in your geographic area. They might agree upon several items that are likely to be carried by the major competitors (Target, if one is located in your area, but other discounters if no local Target exists) and then prepare objective price comparisons between the local stores. Students should also prepare a checklist of items that are contained in the "Guidelines for Growth" to determine how the competitors are handling these policy issues.

ADDITIONAL QUESTIONS

1. Design a research project that will monitor the degree to which the Guidelines for Growth are successful in the perceptions of consumer segments identified in the Guidelines. Compare the competitors.

2. Should Dayton-Hudson try to reach more segments with Target or would it be better to develop additional types of store concepts to reach the additional segments?

3. What kind of training and educational programs would be needed to implement the Guidelines?

4. What kind of logistics system is required to support the Guidelines? What kind of financial information? Outline the basics of a DSS/MIS (Decision Support System, Management Information System) required to support the Guidelines.

ADDITIONAL INFORMATION

Current issues of Business Week, Wall Street Journal, and other trade journals have many articles on the major competitors to Target. Students can be encouraged to examine Business Periodical Index. For additional clarification of lifestyle retailing and the manner in which Target fits into the "portfolio" of lifestyle retailing offerings of Dayton-Hudson (and other examples of this concept), see Roger Blackwell and Wayne Talarzyk, "Life-Style Retailing: Competitive Strategies for the 1980s, "Journal of Retailing (Winter 1983), 7-26.

THE STAMPLER COMPANY[1]

OBJECTIVES

This case presents a situation involving a production-driven, mature company that is wishing to effect a change. Complicating this change process is the fact that demand for their products has been created by customers, not the company.

SUMMARY

The Stampler Company, a family-owned company, supplies hardware to the automobile, recreational vehicle, and mobile home industries. While sales have increased, it has been at the expense of profits. The president and CEO of the company have initiated action to turn around the company and achieve substantial growth.

Among the negative factors are (1) sales are a result of the markets the company was in rather than the company's efforts; (2) preoccupation with the present, (3) a substantial share in present markets; and (4) reliance on a small number of customers.

Of the two company divisions, automotive is the largest. Products such as automobile door-locking systems and air conditioning brackets are made to customer's specifications. Profits are low due to extreme competitiveness. The major questions are: Do we want to make the product? and can we make it for the price suppliers have dictated?

The other division sells products to the mobile home and recreational vehicle markets. These markets are dispersed throughout the United States. Stampler has developed a distribution network to assist manufacturers' reps in serving this market.

Planning for products has considered present manufacturing and marketing capabilities as well as diversification. Lists of possible products have been developed.

QUESTIONS

1. Do you agree with the approach taken by Marks? Explain answer.

2. How would you change a production-driven company to one that is market driven?

3. What products offer the best opportunities for Stampler?

CASE ANALYSIS

---

[1]This teaching note is based on materials prepared by H. Robert Dodge.

1.   Do you agree with the approach taken by Marks?   Explain answer.

The problems encountered have more to do with the implementation of the approach than the approach itself. Marks did not fully discuss the detracting factors. Additionally he should confine the initial discussion to broad product concepts and then proceed to narrow the fields of inquiry.

2.   How would you change a production-driven company to one that is market-driven?

One significant change would be a restructuring of the organization to give greater emphasis to marketing. Another possibility would be to hire consultants to help make the change. Above all, the Stampler Company must develop an incentive system that rewards employees who make suggestions that help the company in marketing its products.

3.   What products offer the best opportunities for Stampler?

Because of their present manufacturing facilities, the least risky and at the same time the best potential would be metal porch and lawn furniture, furniture hardware, and other hardware. It would be a mistake to enter into the plastics markets. The best opportunities would be to buy companies and retain their present managements. In this fashion, Stampler would not have to stretch the capabilities of its present staff with its marketing limitations.

ROCKWOOD MANNER[1]

CASE OBJECTIVES

The purpose of this case is to design a marketing mix for service/product that is marketed to a special market segment, elderly citizens. The case requests that students determine the market potential, design the general nature of the product to be delivered and to decide how the product should be priced. The specific case objectives are:

1. To make students aware of the large and growing elderly population, their aggregate financial strengths and their potential demand for a wide variety of goods and services.

2. To illustrate demand forecasting by applying logic and judgment to secondary data.

3. To show why elderly may choose different living environments when they retire.

4. To make students aware of the unique pricing methodologies in the life care market.

SUMMARY

Rockwood Manner is a retirement facility in Spokane, Washington. Rockwood Manner is a residential/health facility which offers a full spectrum of services to meet the housing, nutrition, health, social, and spiritual needs of older individuals. Residents purchase the privilege of living in the unit of their choice. Prices are based upon the charge for a standard living unit of 300 square feet. Living units may be purchased for cash or under terms of a time payment contract. A minimum down-payment is required for a living unit under terms of the contract. The balance, plus interest on a declining balance, is amortized for a term of 84 months (seven years). In addition, residents pay a monthly service fee.

The market for Rockwood Manner consists of ambulatory citizens who are able to care for themselves at the time of admission. There is a per diem charge for infirmary care beginning with the 11th day of confinement during any one month.

Recognizing the growing demand for retirement housing the board of directors of a nonprofit retirement home has asked the administrator for a proposal to expand existing facilities. The administrator must assess the demand and recommend the type and number of units to be built. He must also recommend a pricing methodology.

---

[1].These teaching notes are based on materials prepared by Professor William R. Wynd, Eastern Washington University.

QUESTIONS

1. Describe the market segments for elderly life care facilities.

2. Speculate why elderly may choose to live in retirement facilities.

3. Estimate potential demand for retirement facilities in Spokane County.

4. What type of facilities should be constructed?

5. How many units should Chapman recommend?

6. What pricing methodology should be used?

1. Describe the market segments for elderly life care facilities.

Life care facilities offer shelter and care for the life of the resident. Nearly all such facilities require that the resident be ambulatory when they enter. When they become disabled, intermediate or more intensive care is provided.

The case hints that the active elderly are not a single unitary market but a segmented market. The most basic segmentation would be those who are ambulatory and those who are restricted to health care facilities. Further the case indicates that there are some individuals who wish to save for an estate for their children while others should spend their hard earned money on themselves. This additional dimension of segmentation that might be utilized in marketing strategy. Facilities vary by the amenities offered. Generally there are two segments: the high end, affluent market and the low end "economy" segment often government subsidized.

2. Speculate why elderly may choose to live in retirement facilities.

Most elderly don't choose to live in retirement facilities. National figures show that only 5-7 percent of the elderly choose that life style. There are several reasons.

Some people depend on others for support. They gain personal strength through friendships. As they age persons in their support group may die or move away causing a gap in their lives. A retirement home, with its congregate living, provides a ready opportunity to develop a new support group.

As age progresses physical ability declines and attitudes change. A house in suburbia with a lawn, garden, and house maintenance may take on a different meaning. Congregate living offers the opportunity to have more free time.

The need for security, in the physical as well as medical sense, increases with age. Both physical security as well as peace of mind in the knowledge that the resident will be looked after until death can be of primary consideration in choosing to live in a congregate life care community. The importance of the "security" dimension probably increases with age.

3. Estimate potential demand for retirement facilities in Spokane County.

Estimating market size:

Annual increase in population 60+ between 70 and 80 = 1000 (from case).

	54,436		- population over 60 in 1980
	5,000		- increase since 1980
	59,436		- population in 1985 if relationship hold true (could also calculate from Figure 1)

5%	6%	7%	Percent of population 60+ living in retirement homes, national study (from case)
2972	3566	4160	Spokane County 60+ living in retirement homes 1985 - projected from national study

1600	1600	1600	Number of elderly actually living in retirement homes includes 80% of those in the infirmary (Text)

1372	1966	2560	Apparent demand not filled

4. What type of facilities should be built?

Rockwood must maintain image--up scale, top of the line.

Elderly want to remain independent as long as possible--facilities should be as near like what they move out of, i.e. single family, no stairs, no yard work-but detached, and space to park R.V.

Cottages probably most closely approximate active elderly's current living environment plus they maintain the up scale "elite" image of Rockwood.

5. How many units should Chapman recommend?

Rockwood should target the market for single family units demanded by the affluent elderly. This is based on the assumption active elderly want to travel and spend their money but don't want to be tied down. If something happens to their health, however, they want to be cared for. They don't want condos or apartments because they are independent--moving into one of these puts them into a group and they have an adverse image of apartments developed over time. But only a small part of the market (probably 10%) have the money to put down for a single family unit.

1372	1996	2560	Apparent demand not filled stated above
-350	-350	-350	Less competition 250 units occupied by 350 elderly (40% by couples and 60% by singles)
1022	1646	2210	Demand
x.40	x.40	x.40	Assume 40% live together as a couple
409	658	884	
2	2	2	Two live together
204	329	442	
20	33	44	Go for the high end of the market - top 10%

I would recommend they start with 25-30 units depending on the most economical way of laying out the development.

6.   What pricing methodology should be used?

The pay as you go method is a risky approach for a new community, especially in an inflationary environment. Increasing fees as the community ages may be beyond the capability of residents on fixed incomes to pay. Inflation simply escalates the increase.

The open-group methodology may be more appropriate if a realistic planning horizon is chosen. This method is more equitable than the pay as you go approach.

Probably the best method is the closed group approach because of its equity. But fees can be substantially greater than the other two approaches. Higher fees, however, are compatible with the upscale elite image Rockwood is projecting. Chapman will have to defend the fees to prospective residents on the basis of equity.

7.   Uses of the Case

As the case states our nation's elderly are increasing in numbers. In the decades to come they will influence the political process because more of them vote. Their purchasing power will increase and their share of total liquid assets held by individuals will be important to the financial community. Young people should be aware of the emerging force. This case sets the stage for developing that awareness.

This case can be used effectively in sections of the course where supply, demand, and price are discussed. Since the decision to build a specific number of units is based on both quantitative and qualitative data this may be an opportunity to point out the importance of qualitative and judgmental input.

Figure 1 shows the population distribution in Spokane County by age groups. One can visualize the population movement over time and project the growing influence of the elderly. An instructor may wish to show the population distribution and projections for his area. These projections are probably available from the County Planning Department.

Additional insights into the complex area of pricing can be obtained from:

Howard E. Winklevons and Alwyn V. Powell, "Continuing Care Retirement Communities: An Empirical, Financial and Legal Analysis." Irwin, 1984.

HOME PRODUCTS UNIVERSAL DEVELOPS DB-14[1]

CASE OBJECTIVES

This case illustrates the problems that may be caused by failure to use the marketing concept in planning a new product. It also provides practice in interpreting marketing research results.

SUMMARY

Home Products Universal is a medium-sized Midwestern manufacturer of household cleaning and maintenance products. The company is able to compete with the giants in the field because of aggressive marketing, high products quality, and an effective cost control program. The quality of the product relative to its competition is assured by regular comparative testing and, if necessary, reformulation. HPU's marketing strategy is essentially defensive, though. The company has never introduced a totally new product, but rather follows the lead of its competition.

Allen R. Scala, HPU's Director of Product Research and Development, wants to see HPU change to a more innovative policy of product development, partly in order to expand the company's operations nationwide. Discussions with Arthur V. Pensa, the Director of Product Marketing, and Alphonso Caravelle, the Director of Manufacturing Operations, encourage Scala to proceed to looking for ideas for new products. With the help of his staff, he comes up with two that seem feasible: a sweeping compound for home use and a powdered laundry bleach. Scala, Pensa, and Caravelle decide to develop only the liquid bleach, based on personal interests and what they think HPU's President, Alfred Knutson, will accept. After ten weeks of development, Scala's department is able to produce a dry bleach that outperforms the liquid product, but is safe for fabrics and hands. At this point, the new product is first revealed to Knutson, who orders market testing of the bleach.

The market testing is referred to Aloysius LaGrange, the Director of Marketing Research. LaGrange conducts two studies: first, a placement test in which housewives are given samples of the powdered bleach to use, then are asked for their reactions to the product; and second, a study of consumer attitude toward and usage of bleach in order to find out how consumers use bleaches and what their perceptions are toward them. When the results become available, Knutson requests a briefing. After the results are presented, he asks Scala, Pensa, and Caravelle to each write a memorandum concerning his recommendations for the future of the new product.

QUESTIONS

---

[1]The content of this analysis has been adapted from the teaching suggestions by William M. Weilbacher, author of the original case in Marketing Management Cases by William M. Weilbacher.

1. Define the "marketing concept." How does the marketing concept relate to the facts presented in this case?

2. Summarize the consumer placement research findings given in Exhibits 1-4 through 1-9.

3. Summarize the usage and attitude research findings given in Exhibits 1-10 through 1-16. What are the implications of these findings for a new product in the bleach market?

4. Home Products Universal's laboratory evaluation of the product DB-14 appears to be contradicted by the consumer research findings. Is it possible that consumers may prefer a product that does not meet the highest performance specifications?

5. Evaluate the memoranda written by Caravelle, Pensa, and Scala in response to Knutson's request. Do you agree with any of these men? If so, tell which one and why. If not, prepare a memorandum to Mr. Knutson that is properly responsive to his request.

6. When Mr. Knutson receives the three memoranda, how should he proceed?

CASE ANALYSIS

1. Define the "marketing concept." How does the marketing concept relate to the facts presented in this case?

The "Marketing Concept" means that the manufacturers' sales success depends upon his ability to make products that consumers want and to provide them at a time, in a place and at a price that satisfies these consumers. The marketing concept implies that the most successful manufacturers will be those manufacturers that most thoroughly understand what consumers do and do not want.

The "marketing concept" may be contrasted with the Manufacturing Concept. The manufacturing concept means that the manufacturer makes what he wants to make, or knows best how to make, or is best situated to make profitably, or what he believes, intuitively, that the consumers want him to make. Under the manufacturing concepts, the presumption is that the manufacturer rather than the consumer knows best what the consumer will want to buy and little or no attempt is made to develop or guide product planning decisions in the light of organized knowledge of consumers.

This case reveals the basic orientation of Home Products Universal's venture into new product development to be toward the manufacturing concept. At least until President Knutson gets into the act. It is he rather than his senior marketing, manufacturing or product development officers that raises the question of whether the consumer has had an opportunity to express his collective attitude toward DB-14. But the product has been brought in a relatively finished form before anyone thinks of finding out what the consumer knows or wants. It is this inward orientation toward the skills of the company rather than outward toward the desires of the consumer that distinguishes the manufacturing concept.

2. Summarize the consumer placement research findings given in Exhibits 1-4 through 1-9.

Exhibit 1-4: All of the consumer testers were asked to rate the new product on a five point scale ranging from Poor through Average to Excellent. 16% of all the testers considered it to be only average or worse. It is difficult to assess figures of this kind in the absence of some kind of reference point or average performance. Although no averages or norms are given in the case, two points can be made:

a) Consumers tend to give favorable ratings to products that are tested monadically or without a specific competitive reference point. It is most unusual for there to be a distinctly higher proportion of consumers in the two lowest scale positions than in the two highest scale positions and extremely unusual for almost half of a testing group to rate a product negatively.

b) Everything that is true of products in general (as just summarized under point a) is especially true of any product that consumers can in any way conceive of to be either new or a departure from tradition. Consumers seem to expect that they should react positively to new products and they do not, as a general rule, let researchers down unless the product is an a-ject failure.

Exhibit 1-5: About one in three testers can find some advantage to DB-14. Two thirds do not believe that the product has any advantage at all.

Among those reporting an advantage, mildness to hands is the most important. All of the other responses have to do with safety, pleasantness, or convenience.

Exhibit 1-6: About three out of four testers believe that the product has at least one disadvantage. And one fourth do not believe the product to have a disadvantage.

The major disadvantages are that the product doesn't get clothes white and that it is not strong enough or is too mild. Fully one half of all testers and two thirds of the total who feel the product has a disadvantage give one or the other of these negatives.

Exhibit 1-7: When the testers are asked to compare DB-14 to their regular liquid bleach product, 72% say they prefer the liquid bleach. Less than one in five prefer DB-14 and 10% express no preference.

Those who prefer their regular liquid bleach product give two reasons in particular for their preference: the liquid bleach gets clothes whiter (72%) or is stronger (64%). Another 31% simply say that the liquid bleach is best for them.

No single reason for preference of DB-14 is given by the small minority that likes it. Good odor, mildness to hands, and mildness to fabric are all given as reasons for preference by a few respondents.

Exhibit 1-8: The testers were asked to express a purchase intention relative to DB-14 on the assumption that it would soon be available in stores. Over half (54%) said they definitely would not purchase DB-14. An additional 33% said they were not sure, or probably wouldn't purchase DB-14.

Although questions or purchase intention cannot be taken as literal predictions of future behavior, they are generally acknowledged to be good measures of consumer attitude. It is unusual to encounter negative purchase intention (attitude) at the levels seen in this study.

Exhibit 1-9: The testers were also asked to estimate the price they might pay for DB-14 were it available in stores. Three quarters of the testers would expect to pay less than for liquid bleach.

Again, the results of price questions of this type cannot be taken literally. At best, they reflect attitude and can be used to pinpoint probably problem areas. In this case almost every respondent suggests that he would not be willing to pay the price that will be asked for DB-14 if it is marketed. (Recall from the case, page 11, that "it could be marketed at a price about 1/3 higher than liquid bleach, on a completed washload basis.")

Summary content. The question that this research poses is how can consumers be so negative in the face of the enthusiasm that exists within Home Products Universal for this product. It is precisely this conflict that defines the marketing concept. And although the case is purely imaginary, the thrust of the facts is totally realistic. Too often management becomes mesmerized by its own expertise and its assorted prejudices and the marketing concepts is ignored. It is precisely this that is often responsible for new product failure, at least in those cases where no marketing research exists or where the research or its interpretation is either inadequate or self serving.

3.   Summarize the usage and attitude research findings given in Exhibits 1-10 through 1-16. What are the implications of these findings for a new product in the bleach market?

Exhibit 1-10: 78% of all households report that they are users of household bleaching products. One out of five of all households are heavy users of household bleaching products when a "heavy user" is defined as a household that consumes more than one quart of bleach a month. Three out of five (58%) of all households are light users of household bleaches in that they use less than one quart of bleach a month.

22% of all households report that they do not use household bleaching products.

Exhibit 1-11: The lower the income of a household, the more likely it is to be a bleach user and the more likely is it to be a heavy bleach using household.

The less well educated the head of household the more likely is the household to use bleach and the more likely is it to be a heavy bleach using household.

The older the head of household the more likely is the household to use bleach and the more likely is it to be a heavy bleach using household.

Bleach usage is fairly evenly spread by geographic area - the area with the highest incidence of bleach usage is the South (88%) and that with the lowest incidence is the Northeast (72%). Heavy users are slightly more likely to be found in the South (24%) and slightly less likely to be found in the North (18%).

Exhibit 1-12: White fabrics are the most likely items to be bleached and white fabrics are bleached with much greater frequency than are non-white fabrics.

Sheets, towels and shirts are the white fabrics most often bleached. Almost everyone bleaches sheets and towels and almost everyone bleaches them every time they are washed. Eight out of ten housewives bleach white shirts and they bleach them about three out of every four times they are washed.

Bleaching of colored, delicate and synthetic fibers has very low incidence and very low frequency.

Exhibit 1-13: Housewives use bleach for two predominant reasons: to get clothes whiter and cleaner.

Exhibit 1-14: Liquid bleaches are believed to do the job, that is, to get clothes whiter, cleaner and brighter. They are also believed to be strong and economical by the strong majority of bleach using households.

Exhibit 1-15: But liquid bleaches are acknowledged to have shortcomings. Half the users of bleaches believe them to be too harsh, either on fabrics (32%) or on hands (26%). One quarter of bleach users say that liquid bleaches ruin colors and that they cannot be used on synthetic fabrics. 22% say that they are clumsy and heavy to carry around.

Exhibit 1-16: An ideal bleach would get clothes clean and white; and it would not cost more than available liquids. A modest minority believe that the product should be safe for colored clothes (22%); synthetic fabrics (16%); skin (8%).

Implications for a new product: Bleach is an old-fashioned product and according to these figures the market is literally dying away. It is a product which, in its conventional form, delivers the goods. No new product is harder to introduce successfully than one that proposes to supplant an accepted standby of the older, less affluent, relatively poorly educated segments of the market. A new bleach product must seem to do the heavy duty jobs of bleaching clearly better than the available chlorine bleaches.

4. Home Products Universal laboratory evaluation of Product DB-14 appears to be contradicted by the consumer research findings. Is it possible that consumers may prefer a product that does not meet highest performance specifications?

The essence of marketing success is corporate responsiveness to consumer wants and to changes in consumer wants. Companies become great because of their ability to produce products that achieve consumer acceptance. As time passes, the original grounds for product differentiation and success tend to become frozen into the company's historic procedures tend to become synonymous with the way in which "good" and"quality" products are made. Standards set as the company comes into maturity become a part of its internal culture, and are perpetuated as the "only" way in which to operate or as the "right" way in which to operate.

But continuing corporate success can only be guaranteed by the evelopment of a flexibility in adapting these established ways of operating to meet changing consumer wants: corporations that do not do this tend to wither as they resolutely defend their historic operating standards. A company has no realistic alternative: it must learn to move with and respond to changes in consumer tastes.

In the case of Home Products Universal, there has been no tradition of moving directly with consumer tastes except through the device of copying or improving upon the successful innovations of competitors. This is a relatively safe and sound corporate policy to follow as long as one has a laboratory that can successfully extend the basic innovations of others, and as long as a company is content to forego the marketing profits that almost inevitably flow to the innovator.

Now, as Home Products Universal moves into a policy of product innovation it almost innocently adopts the classic posture of those manufacturers that adhere to what we have called the Manufacturing Concept. It proceeds on the assumption that it contains within itself the elements of every man and that it, in its own collective wisdom, undertakes to make will reflect its own good judgment about what the consumer needs and will want to buy.

This is classic manufacturers' thinking. The manufacturer can sell only what the consumer will buy. And the consumer is not influenced a whit by engineering considerations, or by rational convictions or by single-mindedness. The consumer wants a variety of merchandise often with seeming perverseness, and in total ignorance of engineering laws and niceties, but almost always within a logic that is straightforward, simple, clear and once understood, wonderful to behold. If the consumer were not the consumer, but rather a rational economic man, singlemindedly pursuing a rational and objective goal - then marketing would not exist, for there would be no need for it.

So, consumers do not always choose products which may be said to meet highest performance specifications and it is for this reason and because consumers almost never reach a consensus as to what "highest performance standards" mean to them, that consumer goods marketing as we know it exists and is important.

5.   Evaluate the memoranda written by Caravelle, Pensa and Scala in response to Knutson's request. Do you agree with any of these men? If so, tell which one and why? If not, prepare a memorandum to Mr. Knutson that is properly responsive to his request.

The three memoranda express three different points of view about the consumer and the link between corporate marketers and the consumer which is provided by marketing research. It is, incidentally, not at all uncommon for indifference to what the consumer really wants and antagonism toward marketing research to appear as different elements in the same point of view. The acceptance of marketing research by a business executive assumes that the consumer may have a unique and unanticipated point of view that is different from that held by the individual executive, or his wife or his associates. This insight is a relatively sophisticated one and not every business executive has it. Simplistic and rather romanticized views of the consumer are most likely to be held by those executives who have least experience in dealing with them and this lack of sophistication is very frequently expressed in contemptuous reactions to marketing research and its findings.

In this case, Caravelle, the Director of Manufacturing Operations, uses the research as an excuse to attack the new product development program. He sees no reason to take the time and spend the money to develop new products when his competitors are already doing the job, at their expense, for him. This is a reactionary point of view, of course, and one that dooms Home Products Universal to the role of follower. Scala's view about the importance of new products to the future of the company is, of course, a much more fashionable view. Whether or not a company with Home Products Universal's philosophy - regional copier of established national brands at high standards of quality - can survive is an interesting question. This trend in many industries seems to be against the survival of such firms.

The Pensa viewpoint is perhaps somewhat more enlightened. He recognizes exactly the nature of the dilemma, but is inclined to believe that it is merely a matter of finding the proper advertising approaches to convince the consumer. Pensa apparently believes that advertising is a rational matter - a kind of public dialogue between the unenlightened consumer and the all-knowing manufacturer. If the right clutch of words can be found by the advertising agency, the consumer will be convinced because of the total rationality and absolute rightness of the case. If this view of advertising is correct, then one must explain why relatively similar products do not always gain equal shares of consumer's expenditures if all of their advertising is basically informative. Market position, of course, depends upon more than advertising: it depends upon product, and promotion, and pricing, and historic product success, and residual advertising caused images and current advertising message, that counts and wins the market place. If the product is incompatible with what the consumer wants, as is DB-14, then advertising is not likely to overcome consumer resistance.

The whole point, of course, is that Pensa assumes that the Home Products Universal product is right and that the consumer is wrong and that it is merely a matter of straightening out the consumer through advertising. But it is not as simple as that. The product, good as it is, is not as simple as that. The product, good as it is, is not what the consumer wants: it is inconsistent with a whole agglomeration of beliefs, attitudes, practices and learning that is real and perhaps insuperable, irrational to Mr. Pensa as it may seem.

The Scala response is the best of the group. It recognizes that both product positioning - that is, what one says about a product - and product performance - that is, what a product does - are important. And it recognizes that both must be responsive to and compatible with what the consumer wants. Scala's revised product positioning reflects the major implications of the research. But he also recognizes that the product may have to be reformulated too, so that it is not, in either physical appearance or activity, incompatible with the spirit of the new positioning.

My own experience with students has been that a goodly proportion will fail to choose the Scala memorandum either because they align themselves with Caravelle or Pensa, or because they dope out another, often quite hairbrained point of view. This student response always dumbfounds and often depresses me until I realize that the notion of the Marketing Concept is often quite difficult to grasp. It is much more profound and subtle than it seems to be, perhaps, and it is an easy notion to accept all marketing decisions. In simplest terms, it might be stated - find out what consumers want, be sure you're right, then give it to them. Perhaps every marketing student should be required to write <u>that</u> on the board one hundred times.

6.   When Mr. Knutson receives the three memoranda, how should he proceed?

Knutson risks revealing his own shortcomings in this situation. He must be smarter than the smartest of his three underlings, or he must at least have confidence in his ability to identify the best of the alternative proposals. He opens himself up to the possibility of a debate over what should be done with DB-14 in which he himself must participate.

One of the prerequisites of a chief executive officer is that he may simply pass judgment without involving himself in the decision-making process. The minute that he puts himself in the role of choosing between his subordinates' viewpoints, he enters the decision-making process as a participant, rather than as a decider.

There is certainly nothing wrong with this - some chief executives even seem to enjoy it. But it is not, by custom, required of our corporate leaders. Knutson has one of several options in dealing with the situations that he has created.

a)   He may issue an executive order, with or without supporting explanation. Such an order may upset and depress those officers whose views it does not represent. If Knutson goes into detail about the course he chooses he may also expose his own ignorance.

b)   He may call a meeting to discuss the best course of action to take, given the points of view expressed. This has the potential hazard, again, of exposing his ignorance. Worse, it involves him in the work of his subordinates and this debases their power, authority and legitimacy. Also, it takes the chief executive away from the things he should be doing. But at least the conference gives his subordinates an opportunity for face-saving.

c)   He can throw the problem back to his subordinates, letting them work out a joint solution for his approval. This puts the various roles back into proper perspective and it is always possible that the men will come up with the right solution. That is, after all, what they are paid to do.

VOLKSWAGEN OF AMERICA[1]

CASE OBJECTIVES

1. To illustrate the concept of brand positioning.

2. To discuss the usefulness and need for consumer research.

3. To investigate the relationship between product positioning and its effect upon marketing strategy.

SUMMARY

Five months after Volkswagen introduced a new car called the Dasher, sales were far below what Volkswagen had originally projected. Extensive data on current Dasher purchasers and car buyers in general have been collected. Volkswagen must now determine why Dasher sales are decreasing. Volkswagen feels that the problem may be in the positioning of the product that was achieved through current advertising and merchandising techniques.

QUESTIONS

1. What can be learned about Dasher's problems from the Tables given in the case?

2. What was the basic positioning error made by Volkswagen with the Dasher?

3. Based on the present positioning of the product, what marketing strategy could you recommend for the product?

4. Do you recommend repositioning the Dasher? If yes, How?

CASE ANALYSIS

1. What can be learned about Dasher's problems from the tables given in the case?

The data show that television was the best advertising medium followed by articles in newspapers and magazines. Although 75 percent of the buyers heard about Dasher on television, a budget allocation of this amount may not leave enough for the print media. The survey also showed that the retail salesperson did hot have a good pitch for the car. They could not counter questions on price and did not seem to know what to stress. Generally the salespeople emphasized economy, size, and front wheel drive. However, the car is not an economy car in size or concept. In addition, the survey showed that

---

[1] Teaching note based on materials prepared by W. Wayne Talarzyk, Rodger Blackwell, and James Engle in Contemporary Cases in Consumer Behavior (Hinsdale, Ill: The Dryden Press, 1985)

prices paid for Dashers were much higher than people had expected to pay for the car. Seems like many people were turned off by the high price.

About 35 percent of the trade-ins for new Dashers were from Volkswagen owners. On the other hand, Fox tended to pull from non-owners of VW. This means that Dashers are drawing from existing VW owners and are merely trading "Beetle" buyers up to the Dasher. Also Dasher attracted few Toyota and Datsun trade-ins suggesting Dasher was not able to compete with these cars on price. Most of the Dasher trade-ins were Fords and this may suggest something about segmentation. The data also suggest that the Dasher was not sold for exterior styling. People did not think the Dasher was as good looking as the Fox.

The Dasher did not sell well to singles, to women, or to young buyers. Most of the buyers were 55 and up. Some students will say this shows the car was correctly positioned and others will point these markets out as opportunities to be exploited.

2. What was the basic positioning error made by Volkswagen with the Dasher?

The Dasher was rushed to market to help stop the decline in market share caused by the inability of the "Beetle" to compete with Toyota and Datsun. Volkswagen management did not have a precise idea who should buy the new car and why. The advertising slogan used for the Dasher "The Perfect Car for Its Time" was vague and meaningless. It appeared Volkswagen was going after the family market for 4-door sedans. However, they also emphasized acceleration from zero to 50 in 8.5 seconds which would appeal to the sports car driver. The ads also emphasized high mileage and the thrifty theme. Other ads stressed the safety features of front wheel drive and skidbreaker. The car appeared to be "all things to all people." Unfortunately the buyers thought the car high priced and this ruined their claims of economy of transportation. Also the car's good acceleration clashed with the dumpy looks and the needs of a family car. Volkswagen did not have a specific market segment picked out and they did not advertise to sell individual buyers.

3. Based on the present positioning of the product, what marketing strategy could you recommend for the product?

The product is currently positioned as basically an improvement upon the "Beetle;" attempting to reach that segment who want more than a "Beetle" but cannot afford the "Audi Fox." The product features which have been focused upon have been contemporary styling, good handling, performance, and economy.

Based on these features which have been emphasized, the marketing mix variables that students should explore are price and promotion. These two variables should reflect these same characteristics.

The data does reveal that consumer's product images are different from Dasher's intended product concept. In addition valuable demographic data is gained on current Dasher purchasers.

4. Do you recommend repositioning the Dasher? If yes, how?

Students will probably recommend that the Dasher be repositioned. An argument can be posited that Dasher is currently positioned in a market that does not really exist (between the Beetle and Audi Fox). Positioning the product as better than one, but not quite the other, can lead to this problem

To reposition the Dasher, some aspect of its marketing mix must be changed. Changing some aspect of the product itself is difficult because of set-up time and tooling costs required. Distribution is predetermined, based on current and existing dealerships. The two variables that appear to have the greatest chance of effecting change are price and promotion.

Price represents one possible variable that could be changed. The purchasing price for over 90% of Dasher buyers had been less than $5250. The Dasher appears to carry a high price image among the buyers. it appears as if non-buyers may not view the extra-product-features as being justifiable through a high price. Although the price could be lowered to achieve a more economical savings image, it is not likely, due mainly to the small margins earned on most compact cars.

Promotion may be changed or increased to position the Dasher more solidly among its competitors. If the promotional budget is increased with no change in strategy, very little will possibly be achieved. Promoting a product more to a non-existent market will not increase the sales. Students should recommend that new promotional techniques should be employed to reposition the product among buyers of Dashers as determined by the demographic data. The ideal Dasher buyer would be the consumer who is married, male, between 25-39, at least a high school graduate, professionally or managerially employed, and earns between $10,000-25,000 annually.

ACTUAL COMPANY DECISION

Volkswagen did not choose to make adjustments downward in the price of the Dasher. In fact, monetary exchange rates made it necessary to raise Dasher prices even higher than ever. Volkswagen attempted to position the Dasher as a high priced family car. Ads were run with high status models and backgrounds to give the car a luxury image. This campaign seems generally to have been a failure. Volkswagen still imports Dashers, but these cars have never sold in high volume. Meanwhile, Volkswagen has introduced two new Audi models (the 4000 and 5000) that have swept the market for high priced family sedans. Unless Volkswagen comes out with a new model, the Dasher appears to be a lost cause.

SEB[1]

CASE OBJECTIVES

1. Illustrates the problems of developing a segmentation and positioning strategy for the second brand in a new market.

2. Provides the opportunity to formulate an entire marketing plan for a new product.

3. Allows students to appraise the advantages and disadvantages of market entry as a number two competitor.

SUMMARY

A major French brewery (SEB) is considering entry into the bottled shandy market. Bottled shandy is a combination of beer and lemonade and SEB's main competitor has the market to itself. SEB has to decide whether to enter the market and if so it has to decide on a marketing strategy (target segments and positioning) and the entire marketing mix (product formulation, price, promotion, and distribution). SEB believes the shandy market will grow, but the firm was taken by surprise and has not had much time for concept development and testing. A decision not to launch in 1980 would allow SEB's competitor to reinforce its monopoly position in this promising market.

QUESTIONS

1. What is the bottled shandy concept?

2. How should SEB segment the market?

3. How should the SEB shandy be positioned?

4. What marketing mix do you recommend?

5. Should SEB enter the bottled shandy market in 1980 and, if so, should they test market the product or go national?

CASE ANALYSES

1. What is the bottled shandy concept?

Shandy is a mixture of beer and lemonade that consumers find thirst quenching and refreshing. Consumers also like the taste and shandy's lightness. Shandy has an image as more adult than soft drinks because of the alcohol content, but less "serious" than beer because the lower alcohol level

---

[1]Teaching note used on materials prepared by Alain Sabathier and Reinhard Angelmar, INSEAD.

and the esence of lemonade. Bottled shandy offers consumers more convenience, but reduces the customer's ability to have it mixed to their own taste. The channel of distribution for bottled shandy would be through supermarkets rather than the taverns where it is mixed to order.

2. How should SEB segment the market?

SEB is interested in who responds best to the shandy concept. They need to know the type of consumers in the potential segments and the size of these segments. The summer 1978 focus group suggested that all adults were aware of shandy, but few young people had heard of it. Thus, if young people were chosen as targets, more emphasis would have to be placed on explaining the shandy concept. The September 1979 focus group showed that the main motivation of shandy drinkers as they are attracted to beer but don't like to drink it. This suggests that present non-consumers of beer or occasional beer drinkers may be good targets. Shandy drinkers are perceived as "dynamic, well balanced, young, sensitive, and up-to-date." Thus, SEB may want to target the product to consumers who want to communicate these characteristics to others.

The 1979 national survey (Exhibit 4) shows some differences in shandy penetration by sex, age, and socio-professional categories. Present shandy penetration is slightly higher among men. On the other hand, some may argue that the shandy image as compared to the male dominated beer image will be more attractive to women. Others will say the greater sweetness will also be more acceptable to women. However, Exhibit 7 shows there is no significant sex difference in preference for the 50-50 or 70-30 varieties among shandy consumers. Also the semantic scale does not show any sex typing. The data seem to suggest there are no strong response differences by sex.

The age data shows the 15-34 group is above average in consumption, while the 45+ groups are clearly below average (Exhibit 4). One reason may be that younger people go to cafe's more than the older consumers. Also the lower alcohol content may make shandy more acceptable to young adults. The 1978 focus grop study suggests greater shandy awareness among older consumers. This implies an even stronger age difference in shandy penetration than the one observed, if we would control for awareness. Thus, it appears that younger consumers respond more favorably to the shandy concept due to lower alcohol and the shandy image.

Shandy has a higher penetration among category C blue collar workers. This may be due to more cafe going among this group or that the greater physical activity compared to other professions leads to greater consumption of thirst-quenching drinks.

Another segmentation bases include geography and time of the year. Right now 60% of PANACH's sales are made south of the Loire river and sales peak in the summer. The major reason shandy may be temperature dependent is it is perceived as a drink which is thirst quenching. A counter-seasonal strategy would have to substitute a temperature-independent benefit in order to succeed.

SEB could also segment the market on the basis of the desired lightness of shandy. The taste tests suggest that shandy consumers differ with regard to the ideal degree of alcohol and lemonade versus beer taste. Among consumers who prefer the light shandy, many have a strong aversion against the heavy shandy. Twenty-one percent among them rate the 50-50 shandy as "awful." Thus, shandy consumers, and perhaps all adult French, differ with regard to shandy lightness and SEB may want to take advantage of this.

To be useful, segmentation criteria must be:

Relevant - different responses to marketing variables
Profitable - segments differ on costs/benefits to enter
Measurable - availability of relevant data on size
Reachable - availability of segment specific channels and media

An evaluation of shandy segmentation criteria is shown in Exhibit 1.

Many different target market strategies can be defined using the segmentation criteria discussed in Exhibit 1. The following three segments are the ones that typically come up during class discussions and are evaluated further in Exhibit 2.

A. Above average shandy penetration segments: Male 15-34 yers, Socio-Professional Category C (workers).

B. Present shandy consumers.

C. Men and women, 15-34 years, category B, C, and D, present shandy drinkers, plus shandy unawares, shandy awares who seek greater convenience, consumers preferring a light shandy, media emphasis on summer month and Southern France.

Criteria for evaluating different target market options would include:

1. Within-homogeneity and across-heterogeneity: people included in the target definition are similar to their response to the major market mix variables; they differ from the excluded people.

2. Completeness: is the target definition sufficiently complete to provide guidance for the main marketing decisions?

3. Implementability: ease of identification of target membership; selective reachability.

4. Competitive activity in segments: possibility to achieve a differential advantage; barriers to entry, substitutes, etc.

5. Segment potential and profitability (present and future).

6. Company target segment fit.

Exhibition 3 provides a comparison of shandy consumption with that of beer, lemonade and soft drinks.

Exhibit 1

EXHIBIT 1

Evaluating Segmentation Criteria

	Sex	Age	Socio-prof'l Categories	Drinking Habits	Geography' Season	Desired Lightness
relevance:						
product	no	?	?	yes (1)	?	yes
commun'ion						
- message	maybe	probably	probably	yes (2)	yes (3)	?
- budget	no	no	no	yes (2)	no	no
- media	yes	yes	yes	?	yes	no
price	?	maybe	maybe	yes (4)	no	yes (4)
distrib'n	?	?	?	some (5)	yes (6)	?
Conclude:	not very relev't	relev't for commun'n	relev't for commun'n	highly relev't	relev't for commun'n & dist'n	relev't for product & price
cost diff.	no	no	no	yes	no	no
measur'v:	yes	yes	yes	some inform'n	yes	some
reach'y:						
- dist'n	?	?	?	some (5)	yes (6)	?
- media	yes	yes	yes	?	yes (6)	?
Conclude:	–	easy to use		self-selection	easy to use	self-selection

(1) If one wants to appeal to beer-drinkers, choice of 50-50; appeal to soft-drink enthusiasts implies 30-70 mixture.
(2) Variations in shandy awareness and beer- vs soft-drink habits imply different communication strategies.
(3) All-year round consumption requires a different positioning than summer and southern consumption (eg, choice of consumption settings).
(4) A light shandy, positioned close to soft-drinks, could be priced higher than a heavy, beer-type shandy.
(5) Possible choice between beer vs soft drink section of supermarkets.
(6) Distribution and media coverage all-year round vs emphasis on summer.

EXHIBIT 2

Evaluations of Three Target Market Definitions

	A Above-avg shandy profile: men, 15-34; workers	B Present Shandy consumers	C Both sexes; 15-34; B,C,D; light preferrers; media: South, summer
within-homog'y:	no: lightness awareness shandy cons	no: lightness age social cat'y	no: social cat'y awareness shandy cons
across-heterog'y:	no: women not very diff't	no: many non-shandy consumers with similar needs but lack of convenience and awareness	yes
completeness: - product	?	?	30-70
- price	?	similar to PANACH' and non-bottled sh'y	closer to soft drinks
- message	difficulty: shandy awares & unawares	heterogeneous target emphasize similarity to non-bottled shandy differentiate vs P.	shandy awares & unawares; social categories emphasize summer context
- media	selective high frequency timing?	broad reach - spill- over important lower frequency timing?	some spillover (heavy vs light) medium frequency timing?
- ad budget	?	?	?
- brand name	CHOPP (young)	CHOPP (suitability)	CHOPP, but: beer- association a pbm
- distribution	?	supermkts, CHR	? soft drinks ?
ease of ID:	yes	yes	difficult: ID of light preferrers
selective reach'y:	yes, probably	difficult	difficult: light preferrers
competition:	different vs PANACH': sex, age, social class	PANACH' has same target definition	different vs P: age, lightness, non-shandy
segmt potential	.48x.39x.3=5.6%	25%	.39(15-34) x .78(B,C,D) x .5(lite pref.) = 15.2%
sales factors: - brand awareness	high (media concentration)	med-low (large target and spillovers	medium
- trial	high (segment- tailored message)	med-high (shandy knowledge)	medium
- repeat	med (taste)	med (taste)	high (product fits segment)
- purchase vol.	?	?	?

EXHIBIT 2 (continued)

	A	B	C
	Above-avg shandy profile: men, 15-34; workers	Present shandy consumers	Both sexes; 15-34; B,C,D; light pre-ferrers; media; South, summer
SEB-target fit: sales objective	110,000 hl	110,000 hl	110,000 hl
segment population	36 Mio x 5.6% = 2 Mio	36 Mio x 25% = 9 Mio	36 Mio x 15.2% = 5.5 Mio
consumption/capita	5.5/1	1.2/1	2/1

EXHIBIT 3

Shandy Consumption Compared to Other Beverages

	PANACH'	BEER	LEMONADE	SOFT DRINKS
1979 Consumption (Mio hl)	0.140	22	3.4	2.9
Penetration	25% (shandy)	56%	35%	27%
Number of consumers	36 Mio x .25 = 9 Mio	36 x .56 = 20.2 Mio	36 x .35 = 12.6 Mio	36 x .27 = 9.7 Mio
consumption/capita	1.6/1	109/1	27/1	30/1

3.   How should the SEB shandy be positioned?

A comparison of alternative positioning bases is given below:

	PANACH'	FOCUS GROUP STUDIES (no segmentation)	SETMENT-ORIENTED (see Exhibit 2)
Positioning bases:			
Functional attributes	convenience (bottle)	refreshing	?
Similarity to other drinks	shandy in cafe	between beer and softs	heavy: beer light: softs
Consumption:			
- when?	?	periods of activity	all yr/summer
- where?	at home	not at home	?/South
- with whom?	?	group	target-dependent
- what context?	?	lively, happy, movement	?
Shandy consumer image	?	dynamic, young,...	target-dependent
Brand image	conservative	cosmopolitan, young, growing,...	target-dependent

4.   What marketing mix do you recommend?

Brand name:

Of the 3 names tested, CHOPP seems to be the best. Might want to consider PANCHO or PACHA for an imitation strategy (names sound similar to PANACH').

The main potential problem with CHOPP is its beer-relatedness, which may go against a positioning close to soft drinks.

Bottle:

Large bottle:
- pros: fits with group consumption; fits with success of 10x25 PANACH' pack; fits with summer - refreshment consumption
- cons: same bottle as table beer - declining market, probably bad image (old-fashioned, lower-class, etc.)

Small bottle:
- pros: same as PANACH' and beer
- cons: no differentiation vs PANACH' and beer

Media:

radio: good for awareness and consumption context
press: visualization; good for targeting

outdoors: visualization; regional targeting possible

Advertising budget:

- competitive parity: same as PANACH'
- objective and task: if target group smaller, can spend less

Product:

30-70: differentiation vs PANACH'; 50% of shandy consumers prefer; no strong aversion against this mixture by the others; probably appeals more to non-beer drinkers and occasional beer drinkers

50-50: same as PANACH'; probably appeals more to beer drinkers

Price:

below PANACH': go for a close-to-beer positioning; target: present shandy consumers

above PANACH': soft-drink-type positioning; target to present non-drinkers of shandy

Distribution:

Emphasis food retailers; since SEB already has CHR sales force, add shandy if no other priorities; but no strong push in CHR.

5. Should SEB enter the bottled shandy market in 1980, if so, should they test market the product or go national?

Entry Decision: Pros and Cons

Consumer demand factors:

Pros -
- interesting market size relative to soft drink and lemonade (PANACH's volume vs Canada Dry)
- interesting market growth
- shandy concept may be a response to the need for a light beer
- shandy has a very positive image

Cons -
- market size very small relative to beer (1983 prediction: 800T hl = 3.6% of beer market)
- existing shandy concept may be an obstacle to positioning for broader penetration and competition against soft drinks

Competitive Structure:

Pros -
- only three competitors; one of the other two is another division (Kronenbourg) of the same group (BSN)

- if SEB does not enter, the shandy market could become a cash cow for the Union des Brasseries

Cons -
- PANACH's brand name provides a significant advantage: identification with the product class
- soft drinks and beer and the generic competitors; both markets are highly competitive

Profitability:

Cons -

- PANACH's pricing strategy does not offer high profitability (4.2F/1.3=3.23F trade selling price - 2F production cost = 1.23F gross margin = 38% of trade selling price), given promotional (6%), sales force (15%), and advertising expenses (17% if same spending as PANACH' in 1979)
- payback is three years at the earliest (production investment between 6 and 7F million), under highly optimistic assumptions (see Exhibit 4 of this note); need to do sensitivity analyses in class regarding the impact of different assumptions.

EXHIBIT 4

Financial Projections: 1980 - 1983

*** SEB Case (Shandy) ***

	Unit	1979	1980	1981	1982	1983	Set:
Total Market	1000 HL	140	300	600	700	800	Mkt Sh
SEB Market Sh	%	0	37.33%	37.33%	37.33%	37.33%	0.373
SEB Sales	1000 HL	0	112	224	261	299	Price:
SEB Price/Lit	FF/L	4.20	4.20	4.20	4.20	4.20	4.20
Factory Price	FF/L	3.23	3.23	3.23	3.23	3.23	
SEB Sales	000 FF	0	36,184	72,369	84,430	96,491	
Production Cost	FF/L	2.00	2.00	2.00	2.00	2.00	
Total Prod. Cost	000 FF	0	22,400	44,800	52,266	59,733	
Gross Margin	000 FF	0	13,784	27,569	32,164	36,759	
Gross Margin	%	ERR	38.10%	38.10%	38.10%	38.10%	Adv
Advertising	000 FF	0	7,000	7,000	7,000	7,000	7,000
Promotion	%	0.00%	6.00%	6.00%	6.00%	6.00%	
Sales Force	%	0.00%	15.00%	15.00%	15.00%	15.00%	
Net Margin	000 FF	0	(814)	5,372	7,434	9,495	
Net Margin	%	ERR	-2.25%	7.42%	8.80%	9.84%	

Fit with SEB

Pros:
- SEB's sales and distribution system fits
- SEB needs to enter growth markets, to compensate for the decline in beer (table beer and 1 litre segments)
- if positioned closer to soft drinks, draw sales from growing soft drink markets, rather than beer

Cons:
- shandy will cannibalize beer
SEB's profitability problems will not be solved by an entry into the shandy market

How should SEB enter the shandy market?

Go National in 1980

Pros:
- benefit from expected market growth
- occupy shelf space
- create brand awareness
- prevent PANACH' from reinforcing his monopoly position in consumers' minds and trade
- occupy the number two spot before Kronenbourg enters

Cons:
- no time to test marketing mix
- risk on market share and financial results

Test-Market

The reverse of the above arguments concerning the national launch.

Sequel

To help students better understand SEB's approach to the Shandy market, we have reproduced a shortened version of the SEB(B) case. The tables have not been included, but students can get a good idea of CHOPP's successes and failures from the text discussion. You might want to hand copies of this out in class when students think they have the SEB case solved. The introduction of CHOPP was quite successful with the brand gaining 24% of a much larger market in 1980. However, this success lead to a serious problem in the form of a third Shandy brand called Force 4. This brand had less alcohol than CHOPP and was positioned more towards the soft drink market. Force 4 was positioned to compete with CHOPP rather than PANACH and in 1981 Force 4 captured 10% of the market and CHOPP's share dropped to 21%. PANACH kept 69% of the market and CHOPP was forced to reposition itself to fight this upstart brand.

SEB (B)*

Late in March 1981, M. Berliot, Product Manager for CHOPP, received the latest pre-test results for the 1981 advertising campaign scheduled to begin two weeks later. It had been decided to maintain the positioning strategy for CHOPP, while improving its advertising execution.

*Copyright c 1984 CEDEP (Centre Europeen d'Education Permanente)
This case was prepared by Reinhard Angelmar, Associate Professor INSEAD-CEDEP, with the assistance of Alain Sabathier, to serve as basis for class discussion. All figures in this case have been disguised.

Berliot was wondering if the proposed 1981 campaign would achieve its objective. After its successful 1980 launch, CHOPP would have to compete in 1981 against a new brand which was also positioned as a thirst-quenching, bottled shandy.

The Shandy Market in 1980

The bottled shandy market more than doubled in 1980, the year SEB's CHOPP bottled shandy came on the market as a second brand, going from 1500 00 hl in 1979 to 382 000 hl. CHOPP's 92 000 hl sales (24% market share) were only slightly below what SEB had hoped to obtain.

A national survey conducted in October 1980 evaluated shandy's overall penetration as being 24%. A total of 48% of shandy consumers had tried bottled shandy and 24% consumed shandy only in this form. Bottled shandy had penetrated particularly among women and teh 45 to 54 age group, while consumers in the socio-professional Category A had rejected it.

When asked why they drank shandy, consumers cited above all its differences relative to beer: it contains less alcohol, is less bitter and more thirst-quenching. However, a considerable number of consumers considered that none of these reasons were important.

In the same way, consumers' opinions varied when asked to position shandy compared with beer and non-alcoholic beverages. The majority of consumers considered shandy as being similar to beer while another group found that shandy was more like non-alcoholic beverages.

The Launching of CHOPP

On April 1, 1980, CHOPP was launched nationwide in the beer section of food stores and in C.H.R. outlets. CHOPP was a mixture of beer (30%) and lemonade (70%) sold in 250 ml bottles with two pack sizes (6/25ml and 10/250ml packs). Its price was set to bring it into line with PANACH'. Taking into account launching promotions, the average price was 4.66 F per litre for PANACH' and 4.55 F per litre for CHOPP.

SEB wanted to position CHOPP as a thirst-quenching drink which resembles beer and can be drunk in all thirst-inducing situations. The brand had to be seen as being "authentic and typically French," in order to distinguish CHOPP from products coming from English-speaking countries. The target market was defined as male, young (under 25), beer and shandy drinkers, and B, C and D socio-professional categories.

The target market and positioning strategies were backed up by the brand name chosen (CHOPP conjures up a beer image), the label and pack design (rounded design and dominant green color are associated with beer), and the advertising copy.

After having consulted three advertising agencies, SEB decided to use TBWA. The advertising campaign comprised several outdoor posters and radio messages which involved thirst-inducing situations with physical exercise (for instance home handymen working, games of table tennis, trekking in the mountains). In the posters, the person was suggested but never shown in his entirety. The punch line was "puts a stop to thirst." The same slogan was used in radio ads. All advertising contained the words (CHOPP shandy) in order to link the brand name to the product class.

CHOPP's 1980 advertising budget was 7.1 million francs, divided into 3.3 million francs for outdoor posters and 3.8 million francs for radio advertising.

PANACH's Strategy in 1980

PANACH' did not change its strategy in 1980 compared with the preceding year. Its advertising budget was increased from 6 million francs in 1979 to 8.4 million francs in 1980 of which 4 million francs were spent on outdoor posters and 4.40 million on radio.

Outcome of the 1980 Campaign

The national survey conducted in October 1980 enabled SEB to measure PANACH's and CHOPP's awareness and brand image among shandy drinkers. Fifty percent of consumers had an unaided awareness of PANACH' compared to 10% for CHOPP. Total awareness was 74% for PANACH' and 25% for CHOPP.

Using 8 semantic scales, the images of the two brands were measured among shandy consumers familiar with these brands. No significant differences emerged.

A study performed in January 1981 among 107 CHOPP consumers and 207 PANACH' consumers supplied information on advertising recall and understanding. Forty-nine percent of CHOPP consumers said that they had seen read or heard CHOPP advertising (total recall). However, only 12% in fact were able to cite elements actually featured in the advertising campaign (proven recall). Of the 49% of consumers who recalled CHOPP advertising, when asked what this advertising was trying to convey, 17% cited the thirst-quenching properties of the product, 14% cited the already-prepared mixture and 12% cited the low alcohol content.

PANACH's total recall was 55% and its proven recall was 22%. Consumers retained above all the already-prepared mixture (17%) and the thirst-quenching nature of the product (11%).

The Competitive Environment in 1981

Given PANACH's satisfactory progress, SEB did not think that U.B. would change its strategy during the coming season.

The main change in the competitive environment during 1981 would be the launch of a third brand of bottled shandy: FORCE 4 by Kronenbourg. SEB knew roughly FORCE 4's strategy through the test market conducted by Kronenbourg during the Summer of 1980.

Like CHOPP, FORCE 4 would be positioned as a thirst-quenching drink. But otherwise, FORCE 4 had a distinctly non-French, soft-drink-type of communication.

NORTH BRANCH PAPER[1]

CASE OBJECTIVES

1. The North Branch Paper case contains a detailed data base for student analysis.

2. Segmentation strategies constitute the theme of the North Branch case, and students are exposed to several potentially significant segmentation alternatives.

3. Brand positioning problems are illustrated in the case.

4. A good example of the difference between perceived and actual product attributes is provided in North Branch.

5. The case illustrates the importance of explicit consideration of future competitive actions in current segmentation decisions.

SUMMARY

North Branch Paper is a division of the American Food Products Corporation. The company was recently acquired in an effort to gain entry for ARP in high margin, nonfood business through established channels. Data from a panel study are given in the case concerning the performance of Countess paper towels. North Branch is involved in an effort to determine whether or not they should go national with the Countess brand and, if so, how.

QUESTIONS

1. Have the Countess marketing efforts been effective in establishing brand awareness?

2. What level of brand preference for Countess has been established?

3. Should Countess attempt to appeal to a particular market segment? (Perhaps segments might be defined by demographics or by extent of paper towel usage.)

4. Should attention be given to changing any specific product attributes of Countess?

5. Should the "cents-off" deal be offered again?

6. What attributes of Countess should receive particular emphasis in a new promotional campaign?

7. Is the Countess brand ready for national promotion?

---

[1]Teaching note based on materials prepared by Fred Kraft.

CASE ANALYSIS

1. <u>Have the Countess marketing efforts been effective in establishing brand awareness</u>?

The case indicates that very little promotional attention had been given the Countess label prior to the acquisition of North Branch by American Food Products in 1970. Dan Orr began managing the brand in 1971, and it was at his direction that the 18-week longitudinal panel study was conducted. From data collected in that study the following exhibit has been prepared.

Exhibit 1

Brand	Percent Mentioned First	Percent Favorite Brand	Percent Most Recent Purchase	Percent of Market
Bouquet	22.7	21.2	24.2	25.0
Laddy	36.4	20.5	22.7	22.0
Vera	11.4	6.8	10.6	16.0
Regal	8.3	5.3	9.1	12.0
Softex	NA	NA	NA	9.0
Countess	12.1	10.6	9.1	6.0
Old South	3.0	0.8	3.8	4.0
Tuffi	3.0	9.1	6.1	2.0
Conserve	NA	NA	NA	---
Can't Remember	2.3	2.3	2.3	---

Discounting promotion prior to 1971, it is clear that a significant level of brand awareness has been achieved during the one year Orr has been brand manager. Countess was mentioned first by 12.1 percent of the participants and was considered the favorite brand by 10.6 percent of the panel. These levels compare very favorably with the performance of the established brands in the study.

2. <u>What level of brand preference for countess has been established</u>?

Countess was the stated brand favorite with 10.6 percent of the sample, and only two brands (Bouquet and Laddy) did better in this regard. Interestingly, however, is the fact that Countess ranked 5th in sales for the 18-week study. This is perhaps an indication of distribution problems, promotions by other brands, or an unfavorable price for Countess. The relationships between market share and price are shown in Exhibit 2. Note that as the price goes from 34.4 cents per 100 feet to 37.5 cents the market share increased, indicating a positive sloping demand curve. On the other hand, market share also increases as the price declines from 34.4 cents per 100 feet, indicating a negative sloping demand curve. These data suggest that there are two groups of buyers. One economy-minded group buys Laddy and Softex, the other buys Bouquet, Vera, and Regal because of the high price or for other reasons. Note that although Countess had an average price, it was ranked 7th on economy. On the other hand, Bouquet ranked third on economy, even though it was the highest priced regular brand. Bouquet appears to be doing something right with its advertising and personal selling efforts.

Countess would seem to have the choice of cutting price to compete with Laddy and Softex or increasing promotional and distribution to compete with Bouquet. North Brand Paper could make very effective use of some advertising expenditure and distribution data on its competitors.

Exhibit 2

Brand	Price/100 ft. (cents)	Market Share (percent)
Tuffi (4-ply)	91.0	2
Bouquet	37.5	25
Vera	37.4	16
Regal	36.0	12
Conserve	34.4	2
Countess	33.9	6
Old South	32.5	2
Laddy	31.3	22
Softex	31.2	9
Average price excluding Tuffi	34.2	

3. Should Countess attempt to appeal to a particular market segment/ (Perhaps segments might be defined by demographics or by extent of paper towel usage.)

Exhibit 3 shows what one student was able to derive from data given in the case. A search for significant demographic and/or usage characteristics for segmentation purposes did not reveal very much. It does appear that with "heavy" users the wife is more apt to be at home (using paper towels perhaps) then with the rest of the sample. Also the "heavy" user seems to have more education and a higher income. A more detailed analysis of the demographic data may provide some additional hints about possible segmentation strategies. In this case, the experience of searching through the data for possible consumer segments is more important than the actual findings that may result.

4. Should attention be given to changing any specific product attributes of countess?

Exhibit 3 in the case shows that Countess ranked 5th on absorbency, 6th on strength, 4th on color, and 7th on economy out of 9 brands in the attitude study. Note that the two leading brands (Laddy and Bouquet) were more consistent on these dimensions than Countess. In addition, data on the importance of product attributes to consumers is given in Exhibit 2 of the case. There it is learned that color is significantly less important than absorbency, strength, and economy. Countess has perhaps placed too much emphasis on color in prior promotional efforts. Moreover, Countess is in the middle of competing brands with respect to these product attributes as revealed by the panel data. Note that Tuffi ranked 1st on both absorbency and strength (the two most import product attributes) and 2nd on color, but it shows a low market share (2%) -- possibly due to the perception that it is not a good value.

These findings indicate that the high-quality, high-priced market segment is quite small compared to the overall, economy-conscious market. The Countess brand manager should find these data useful in attempting the market positioning of the paper towel.

Exhibit 3
(place here)

5.   Should the "cents-off" deal be offered again?

The Fort Wayne panel data indicate the following:

Month	1	2	3	4	5
Countess Sales	15	6	7	11	0

The exact time of the 7-cents-off coupon campaign is not known; however, the surge in the first month's sales suggest that it was then. This may account for Countess obtaining a higher than expected brand awareness and preference. If this assumption is correct, a repeat of the deal seems appropriate.

6.   What attributes of countess should receive particular emphasis in a new promotional campaign?

The panel data indicate that Countess should receive less promotional attention on color and beauty and more attention on strength and absorbency. The value of Countess as a good buy should be stressed. Of course, this is all easier said than done, but many students enjoy creative thinking about how this message could be promoted.

7.   Is the Countess brand ready for national promotion?

American Food Products obtained the North Branch Company because it desired entry into the high-profit, non-food markets through established channels of distribution. Paper products constitute a logical choice for this segmentation strategy.

Whether or not the Countess brand is ready for national promotion depends on a number of factors, some of which are out of the control of AFP. The market is attracting many competitors, and their actions could lead to price cutting and heavy promotional requirements. The showing of Countess in the Fort Wayne panel study indicate that it is a mediocre candidate with good potential. Further delay, however, will not enhance the brand's chances of success on a national basis.

METROPOLITAN CABLE TELEVISION COMPANY (A)

CASE OBJECTIVE

This case focuses on selection of a research design for a research project and on determination of the associated sampling plan.

CASE SUMMARY

Dave Chambers is the marketing manager of MetroCable, a cable television company which serves approximately 100,000 customers in Orange County, California (south of Los Angeles). Over the past few years Metro's customers have leveled off, it's market penetration has slipped and its customer turnover rate has increased. Although an exclusive cable supplier, Metro is now confronted with competition from over-the-air pay television, which competes directly with its Home Box Office (HBO) subscription service. Chambers has elected to conduct a research study to evaluate customer attitudes regarding programming and promotion activities. He now needs to decide how the study should be conducted.

CASE QUESTIONS

1. What are the relative advantages and disadvantages of using mail or using telephone surveying in this situation?

2. How should Chambers go about selecting the sample accounts from the MetroCable computer file?

3. If he were to conduct a mail survey, how could Chambers estimate the number of accounts to select?

4. What additional information could Chambers gain from surveying non-customers in addition to current subscribers?

CASE ANALYSIS

1. What are the relative advantages and disadvantages of using mail or using telephone surveying in this situation?

   Advantages of mail
   a)   cheaper
   b)   can collect greater amount of information
   c)   low interviewer error
   d)   anonymity of respondent

   Advantages of phone
   a)   faster
   b)   probing of answers possible
   c)   more sampling control
   d)   reduces understanding bias
   e)   higher response rate

2. How should Chambers go about selecting the sample accounts from the MetroCable computer file?

Chambers could use simple random, systematic or stratified sampling in this case. Only stratified sampling will insure that roughly 100 HBO customers are included in the final sample. The selection of the individual customers could probably be done by either random or systematic selection from within the selected strata. If systematic sampling is used Chambers must take care to investigate how the computer file is organized.

3. If he were to conduct a mail survey, how could Chambers estimate the number of accounts to select?

He needs to estimate response rate for the survey. For a mail survey this will be affected by questionnaire length and difficulty, sponsorship, interest and use of incentives. Chambers could conduct a limited pilot study to estimate response rate or he could use prior experience judgment.

4. What additional information could Chambers gain from surveying non-customers in addition to current subscribers?

Non-customers would include those who have never subscribed to metroCable service and those who were previous subscribers. The first group could provide information which could potentially help Metro increase market penetration. Prior customers could provide information to help explain and, hopefully, minimize customer turnover rate.

HAMILTON POWER TOOLS (A)

CASE OBJECTIVES

Two main objectives can be pursued by using this case. The first involves determination of the necessity of exploratory research, especially the use of thematic apperception tests (T.A.T.). The second is to present the results of T.A.T. It is useful to identify these students and to direct a dialogue between pro and con forces. The main issue is to determine if the T.A.T. is a valid and reliable form of research.

SUMMARY

Hamilton Power Tools acquired a small industrial chain saw producer in 1949 to broaden its product line. Consumers as well as industrial buyers began to purchase the saw. Eighteen years later, Hamilton decided to investigate its consumer chain saw market and hired a marketing research consulting firm to conduct a consumer survey.

The consulting firm suggested the use of a thematic apperception test (T.A.T.) in exploratory research on chain saw buying motives. The questions concerned what they thought was taking place in each picture. The test was designed to allow people to project their own personalities into the situations presented.

The results of the study indicated, among other things, consumers' perceptions of chain saw users, questions about operating the equipment, worries about cost and safety, and feelings after purchase or use. The firm's head, Mr. Hamilton, was impressed by the results of the study, but questioned how the findings could be used to enhance profits.

QUESTIONS

1. How should Mr. Conway and Gabbins respond to Mr. Hamilton's question?

2. Is Hamilton investigating the casual-user market segment correctly?

3. What conclusions would you draw from the thematic apperception test? Do you feel that this is a valid and reliable test?

4. What specific recommendations would you make to Mr. Campagna concerning the causal-user chain saw market?

ANALYSIS

1. How should Mr. Conway and Gabbins respond to Mr. Hamilton's question?

Mr. Gabbins' question assumes an immediate short-term and direct profit resulting from the research. Mr. Conway should explain that this is a first and vital preliminary step to understanding what makes the consumer tick. Mr. Conway should indicate that the results from this exploratory study can be quantified in the future research. Hopefully, by better knowing the consumer,

Hamilton will keep abreast of the market and be better able to act rather than react to changes in the markets.

2.   Is Hamilton investigating the casual-user market segment correctly?

The thematic apperception test is one of many exploratory research techniques. Focused group interviews, depth interviews, other projection techniques, etc., all might be utilized to gain insights regarding consumer's behavior. The thematic apperception test is a projection technique where the respondent does not have to "embarrass" himself, or lie about the true answer. He need not worry that the interviewer would have a lower opinion of him if he responded in his own person. The concept behind the thematic apperception test is that if a person is given a mask he will tell the truth.

However, one must always remember that exploratory research, especially research in this case, is usually conducted with a small sample size, one that may not necessarily be representative of the total population. The thematic apperception test is a beginning but not the final research technique that should be utilized. Mr. Conway and his associate from Consumer Metrics have not pointed out the limitations of thematic apperception tests. They should do this.

3.   What conclusions would you draw from the thematic apperception test? Do you feel this is a valid and reliable test?

One of the main conclusions from this thematic apperception test is that chain saws are seen as one of the several means of cutting or pruning trees. The firm in the case (Hamilton is a fictitious name) was wrong in thinking that they should exclusively compete directly with their other brand competitors. They often forgot that a large number of potential customers would rent the chain saw or use a handsaw. Hence, they learned they must still promote the generic concept.

Men considering chain saws seem to have two subconscious fears. The first is the concern about the investment in the chain saw. This is indicated in the first two pictures as well as in the last. The men, perhaps, Walter Mittys, were worried about their wives' opinions of them spending a large amount of money on a power tool. The third picture indicates a clear-cut fear of bodily harm that might be caused by using a chain saw. This illustrates the value of a thematic apperception test. Many men, concerned with their macho image, would not directly indicate that they were afraid to use chain saws. Nevertheless, when asked about a third person, we find out that men see the chain saw's blade as something which may cause apprehension. Incidentally, the cutting portion of the chain saw is technically the saw chain which runs around a guide bar. Here we found the incorrect terminology of "blade" being utilized by customers. The term "blade" has certain symbolic overtones. Another conclusion that we could draw from the findings is that the value of the chain saw and the opportunity to do it yourself may be an important motivation to purchase the tool. This concept of pride of ownership and approval from others, especially the wife, was actually used in a promotional campaign by the firm manufacturing these chain saws.

4.   What specific recommendations would you make to Mr. Campagna concerning the casual-user chain saw market?

There are a number of recommendations that students can make concerning this case. One might be that the safety of the chain saws should be pointed out. This might be done in a very subtle way, as increasing the fear of harm in an ad may scare away certain consumers. Giving better training to the store personnel who demonstrate the chain saws might alleviate many of the consumers' fears.

Another recommendation might be to develop some advertising copy based on the "do it yourself" theme or the "she'll be proud of you" theme; then find out if these are effective concepts. It should be remembered that this research is explanatory. The results of this study should be incorporated into additional research.

HAMILTON POWER TOOLS (B)

CASE OBJECTIVES

The prime objective of this case is to present the results of a typical descriptive survey and to have the student make inferences concerning market segmentation and shopper behavior. The secondary objective is to have the student evaluate the sampling technique used in this survey research.

SUMMARY

The Hamilton Power Tools Corporation is primarily involved in an industrial tool and construction market. Their first attempt at consumer marketing research has been conducted by outside consultants. The survey was conducted on the west coast, the company's fastest-growing market, from a list of recent purchasers of Hamilton chain saws.

The typical purchaser of Hamilton chain saws tends to be an older man with a better-than-average income and who has graduated from high school and often has attended college.

Retail activity indicates that the chain saw is a shopping good, that Hamilton does not appear to have extremely high pre-purchase brand loyalty and that the dealer's influence, perhaps to switch over to Hamilton, is great.

QUESTIONS

1.   Why would a company, such as Hamilton, wait so long before conducting consumer research?

2.   Evaluate the sampling frame used by Consumer Metrics.

3.   Develop a marketing plan based upon the information provided in the case.

4.   What further information would be needed before a complete plan could be submitted to Hamilton's management?

CASE ANALYSIS

1.   Why would a company, such as Hamilton, wait so long before conducting consumer research?

Even though the marketing concept has been well accepted in academic circles since World War II, there are still many firms which have not completely adopted the marketing concept. This is particularly true in industrial marketing, where personal selling tends to dominate marketing activities. In industrial marketing, the company usually has a limited clientele whose needs can be informally monitored and served, using salesmen to provide indirect feedback of the customer's opinions. Also, Hamilton has been satisfied with its chain saw sales, and has seen no reason to change its strategy. The company's top management seems not to appreciate the potential for greater sales if they would tailor their chain saw marketing to the needs of the largest market segment, the non-industrial users.

In Hamilton's case, the conservatism of top management is a major factor in their slowness to adopt a consumer-oriented marketing strategy. It seems that the company was founded in the 1940's by John Hamilton, Sr., and he remains in charge. He is comfortable with the industrial market and the marketing methods that he has found successful there. It is evident that he was reluctant to approve the market research project, and would never have initiated it on his own. If the firm is really to become marketing-oriented, rather than sales-oriented, Mr. Campagna and his associates will have to persuade Mr. Hamilton that such a change will really benefit the firm.

2.   Evaluate the sampling frame used by Consumer Metrics.

The objective of the survey is to provide a profile of Hamilton chain saw owners. A survey generated from warranty cards is an efficient way to develop such a profile. Most purchasers of a product as expensive as a chain saw could be expected to return the warranty card. If Consumer Metrics had tried to locate Hamilton saw owners by other methods, say a random sample of all households in a given area, they would have spent more money and located fewer people who owned any chain saw, let alone a Hamilton.

One problem with interpreting the results could be the low response rate. Although it was good for a mail survey, it was still less than 50%, which makes a large nonresponse error likely. One possibility is that the high socio-economic level of the respondents came because few lower-income, less-educated owners of Hamilton chain saws returned their surveys. Another possibility is that people who especially liked or disliked their Hamilton chain saw would be more likely to return the survey than those whose feelings were lukewarm. These possibilities would produce serious doubts about the validity of the results unless Consumer Metrics had made some effort to determine the magnitude of the nonresponse error.

A final consideration is the very limited geographic range of the sample. California is not typical of the whole of the country, and is also a typical market for Hamilton chain saws. Apparently there are market factors there that don't exist elsewhere, and lack of any comparative data from Hamilton's less ideal markets could be a serious limitation to the study if Hamilton uses it as the basis for a nationwide marketing plan.

3.   Develop a marketing plan based upon the information provided in the case.

This is an open-ended exercise, and quite a variety of individual responses could be expected. The information from the survey will be most useful in planning for promotion and distribution, and not very useful for price and product.

Three major types of promotion suggest themselves: in-store advertising materials, other advertising aimed at the target market, and trade sales promotions. Table XV shows that about half of the respondents became aware that a store carried chain saws because of previous visits, while no other information medium had informed more than 20% of the respondents. Table XIV and the discussion of it shows that many of the consumers' initial visits to the stores looking for chain saws were passive ones, with no interaction with a salesman. Thus both attention-getting displays and take-home brochures could be used effectively. The content of the advertising should stress providing information about chain saws in general, as well as Hamilton chain saws, because many respondents were not thoroughly familiar with chain saws when they started shopping for them (Table X). Because the target market is fairly well-educated, and because chain saws seem to be a shopping good, the copy should probably stress rational appeals, not emotional ones.

Table XV does show that 20% did find out that a store carried Hamilton chain saws from magazine, newspaper, radio, or TV advertising. There is no indication of how many more became aware of the Hamilton brand name, but not a particular store, from advertising. Hamilton has been generally ignoring consumer marketing, and has not been aware who might purchase a chain saw in response. Thus, Hamilton could stand to gain from improving or increasing their advertising efforts, aiming them at men between 35 and 50, with at least a high school education, with above-median incomes, and in skilled trades or white-collar jobs. (Tables I-IV). Some students will probably suggest which media should be employed, or even particular magazines or television shows that could reach this segment.

Finally, trade sales promotion could be very important to Hamilton. Tables XI and XII indicate that most of the people who bought Hamilton chain saws had another brand in mind when they first considered chain saws. Table XIII indicates that the dealer had a considerable influence over what saw the customer eventually bought, and Table XIV indicates that most store visits included interaction with a salesman. Since Hamilton has not been actively seeking consumer sales, the dealers may be recommending Hamilton chain saws because they find the quality to be good, and they expect their customers to be satisfied with them (this is consistent with the results reported in Table V). However, Hamilton could probably improve sales by using a "push" strategy, giving the dealer an extra economic incentive to sell Hamilton's product, not another. Such tactics as sales contests, quantity discounts, dealer and salesman education, cooperative advertising, and dealer listings in Hamilton's advertising could be effective to increase the dealer's support for Hamilton products.

On the distribution variable, Table VI shows what kinds of stores generated most of the sales of Hamilton chain saws. Students may suggest concentrating efforts on these stores, or may recommend improving sales from the types of stores which contributed less. Since chain saws are a shopping good, Hamilton should concentrate on developing key dealers in each market, rather than trying to put their product in every possible store in the market. This should help Hamilton's ability to service their dealers, and should not result in much less consumer exposure, since people usually shop around several stores and compare products before buying a chain saw.

4.   What further information would be needed before a complete plan could be submitted to Hamilton's management?

This question may overlap to some extent with question two. Students may mention here a need for a better geographic coverage, or some effort to overcome the deficiencies with the sample already used. One need beyond the objective of the previous survey is to find out how purchasers of other brands of chain saw differ from those who bought the Hamilton product. The data presented here says something about customers persuaded to switch from another brand, but nothing about those who planned to buy a Hamilton but were persuaded to purchase some other chain saw. In addition, Hamilton's management needs to know if they're actually catering to a minor segment of the chain saw market and missing a real opportunity elsewhere.

Some students may also point out the need for more information on the product and price variables, and also the need for the sort of information that is provided by the TAT results in Part B of this case.

SUNCOAST NATIONAL BANK[1]

CASE OBJECTIVE

The objective of this case is to simulate the use of a focus group study for a marketing research problem. Students should gain insight into how a focus group study is conducted and into the analysis of the results. The case serves as an excellent role-playing situation, with students reading the statements of the participants.

SUMMARY

The marketing staff at Suncoast National Bank in San Diego is impressed with the area's future growth potential. Recognizing the success that banks in other areas have had with newcomer marketing programs, the staff would like to design such a program for Suncoast, with the anticipation that it would help increase the bank's share of new area residents. An integral part of the program would be a package of information that Suncoast would provide which could help minimize the inconveniences associated with moving.

QUESTIONS

1. What kind of information should Bennett attempt to get from banking industry sources about newcomer programs?

2. Do you think that it was wise to have a group with both men and women included and with participants of various ages?

3. Did the moderator do an adequate job of getting at the information needed by Bennett?

4. Analyze the focus group transcript very thoroughly. Make a list of problems generated and ideas for the proposed newcomer kit.

CASE ANALYSIS

1. What kind of information should Bennett attempt to get from banking industry sources about newcomer programs?

Bennett should try to find out how the programs operate. For example, who were the target customers? What were the sources of names used? Did they get referrals? Were consumers contacted directly or major employers or both? Next, he needs to know what constituted the program, in particular what information was provided to the newcomers. Last, he should assess the impact that these programs have had and, if possible, their cost to the banks.

2. Do you think that it was wise to have a group with both men and women included and with participants of various ages?

In most cases focus groups are screened to have fairly homogeneous

---

[1] Teaching notes prepared by Donald Sciglimpaglia.

In most cases focus groups are screened to have fairly homogeneous participants. For variety, the number of groups is increased. If budget is a major concern, a smaller number of groups is used but the group might contain more of a cross section of the target population.

In this particular instance we can probably sort out the concerns and opinions of different kinds of people (e.g., student vs. housewife). However, it probably would have been better for the groups to have been more finely broken down, if the budget permitted. For example, a husband will typically view moving to a new community different than his wife. The importance of information will depend on the roles played in the move.

3. Did the moderator do an adequate job of getting at the information needed by Bennett?

Paula Jackson, the moderator, did not do a very outstanding job. For one thing she never adequately got the group to talk about planning the move (where much information is needed) or about how problems could have been corrected. Very little was learned about how the group members selected an initial bank (except Roger who moved a fairly short distance). Lastly, little was learned about the role that other organizations could play in minimizing inconveniences.

The moderator did not do an adequate job of directing the discussion or in following-up on responses. Fortunately, the group was fairly vocal on its own.

4. Analyze the focus group transcript very thoroughly. Make a list of problems generated and ideas for the proposed newcomer kit.

Below is a partial list:

Problems	Ideas
1. claims against movers	claim forms; numbers to call to initiate claims
2. broken furniture	list of furniture repair shops in city
3. locate shopping areas	list of shopping centers and their location; major stores and supermarkets
4. locate schools	list of schools in the area and school boundaries
5. initiate utility services	list of local utilities, new service regulations and key phone numbers
6. drivers license and automobile registration	statement of current state policy, key phone numbers and addresses
7. locate housing	list of realtors, apartment locator services, apartment complexes

The problems associated with check cashing and account verification are more complex. The newcomer could set up an account at Suncoast prior to the move (if possible) and would have a local account with a check guarantee card already established. Or, Suncoast could expedite verification of funds to minimize the clearing time before cashing a check.

EPILOGUE

Redmund and Bennett did not feel that they had learned enough from the focus groups to eliminate the need for conducting the survey. A mail survey was conducted of newcomers which confirmed some of the problem areas suggested in the groups and which suggested other areas as well (e.g., dining guide). A newcomer kit was designed which was used to motivate consumers to come in to visit the local Suncoast branch in their area. New account personnel were trained to pay particular attention to the needs of newcomers and to act as a source of information. The program has met with good success and is currently in operation at the bank.

HAMPTON MAYORAL SURVEY[1]

CASE OBJECTIVES

1. To provide students with an opportunity to evaluate a complete marketing research project from problem conceptualization through analysis and interpretation of findings.

2. To acquaint students with the complexities and uncertainties involved in interpreting survey data containing a moderately high percentage of undecided type responses and non-respondents.

3. To develop student's marketing research skills and to provide them with an opportunity to apply these skills to a typical marketing research situation involving the marketing of a political candidate.

SUMMARY

This case requires students to both assess the research methodology and interpret the findings of a marketing research survey designed to predict the results of a mayoral election. The case begins by describing the present situation and establishing the need and purposes of a proposed telephone survey. Early in the case a controversy arises concerning the selection of an appropriate sampling frame and the determination of the sample size. Two approaches are described and, at the end of the case, the students are directed to evaluate the appropriateness of the selected sampling approach. Detailed findings of the telephone survey are presented in the case and the students are directed to analyze the findings and to evaluate the relationship of these findings to the established purposes of the study. The issues of how to evaluate a probability sample containing a relatively high proportion of non-respondents and undecided respondents are also raised. This case provides an excellent opportunity for students both to apply research principles they have learned in buyer behavior, marketing research, and statistics courses and to further develop their analytical skills.

QUESTIONS

1. Was the sampling methodology (frame, size selection process) that Joe Meyers used better than the methodology that John Adams preferred?

2. Evaluate the questionnaire used in this study. Did it provide answers to the research Questions? Was any pertinent information lacking which you feel should have been included? What questions, if any, would you have deleted or changed?

---

*This case was prepared by Dr. Robert J. Listman of Valparaiso University as basis for class discussion rather than to illustrate effective or ineffective research practice. Copyright c 1985 by Dr. Robert J. Listman. Used by permission.

3. Explain why the findings of this study could or could not predict the results of this election? Do you agree with Adam's conclusion concerning: (a) the election outcome; (b) the assumed patterning of non-respondents' opinions; and (c) the selection of specific precincts for the promotional blitz?

4. Identify any additional analysis of the findings which you believe should be made in order to measure the predictability of this study.

CASE ANALYSIS

1. Was the sampling methodology (frame, size selection process) that Joe Meyers used better than the methodology that John Adams preferred?

    Joe Meyers had the preferred sampling frame because John Adams's selection of the local telephone directory was merely a non-profitability convenience sampling approach. Therefore, this sampling frame would not have been a representative assessment of voter behavior regardless of any substantial increase in sample size. Meyers's stratified random sampling of registered voters was a probability sampling design which would allow specific inferences to be made about the surveyed population. Also, the stratification of the sample by precinct would be more statistically efficient than a simple random sample.
    Of course, any substantial increase in sample size could result in greater statistical precision, but whether that would be worth the additional cost is the question. The assumed 45/55 split in voter preference of the two candidates indicates a heterogeneous population. Therefore, in order to decrease the range of sampling error, a much smaller standard error of proportion would have to be selected. If a standard error of $\pm$ 3 percent at the 90 % confidence level were selected, the sample size would have jumped to over 800. A sizable increase of even 200 additional registered voters would only lower the confidence range to $\pm$ 3.4 %, which is hardly worth the added expense. Consequently, Joe Meyers would not have accomplished much by any moderate increase in sample size.
    Some students may recommend that the sample be additionally stratified by political affiliation. Since the vast majority of voters do not vote a straight party ticket, this additional degree of stratification would add little to the statistical efficiency of the sample.

2. Evaluate the questionnaire used in this study. Did it provide answers to the research Questions? Was any pertinent information lacking which you feel should have been included? What questions, if any, would you have deleted or changed?
    The questionnaire did provide answers to the three, key research questions which were identified earlier in the research process. The questionnaire was pre-tested and appeared to be free from ambiguities, order biases, and poorly worded and unnecessary questions, which indicates that it is a reasonably sound survey instrument. However, a possible weakness is that Question One specifies the reasons which could influence a person's vote. Two important questions to ask the class are: (1) Are these four reasons the only important reasons affecting voter behavior or merely Adams's preconceptions of influencing reasons? (2) Is there really a meaningful

distinction between the importance of primary and secondary reasons in terms of influencing a person's vote?

The appropriateness of addressing a respondent by name when conducting a political poll is also an important issue to raise in class discussion. Should the pollsters ask to speak to an identified registered voter, or should they ask to speak to any registered voter in that household and, thereby, incur the unquantifiable probability of surveying individuals who are not eligible to vote? Class discussion of this issue can be useful in teaching students that there is no one correct answer to this ubiquitous problem of identifying versus not identifying survey respondents.

The questionnaire, as it presently is constructed, takes about three to four minutes to complete which is quite reasonable for this type of polling and certainly less expensive that lengthier questionnaires. However, it is common to find that approximately 80 % of all registered voters state they will vote in an election when in practice only 60 % of the registered voters do vote. Therefore, the issue is, should the questionnaire be lengthened to include three or four filtering questions designed to more realistically identify those that will versus those who will not vote. These questions could add an additional two to three minutes to the survey which could very possibly result in an increase in the number of non-respondents. The survey cost would, therefore, increase because of both the length of the interview and the increased number of calls.

This tradeoff issue of cost versus increased sampling accuracy should be discussed in class because the potential for a severe sampling error is present. This issue was explored with the client buy severe budgetary restrictions caused him to opt for the shorter questionnaire. If the instructor wishes to further discuss this issue in class, it would be helpful to assign the article, "Producing More Accurate Projections With Consistency Filtering Techniques," Marketing News, Jan. 6, 1984, page 16. This article discusses one approach to calculating a filtering index suitable for reclassifying survey respondents. This will help the students to conceptualize some possible filtering questions.

3. Explain why the findings of this study could or could not predict the results of this election? Do you agree with Adam's conclusion concerning: (a) the election outcome; (b) the assumed patterning of non-respondents' opinions; and (c) the selection of specific precincts for the promotional blitz?

This findings indicate that both candidates have approximately the same percentage of registered voters that prefer them. Adams's conclusion that Wagner will win by a narrow margin is merely speculative wishing. The findings indicate that Wagner is leading by only 3% with 21% of the sample undecided or unwilling to state an opinion. Therefore, the assumed proportional split of 45/55 is just an assumption because the data indicates a three-way multinomial dispersion. The sample has to be increased in order for a statistical inference to be made at the predetermined confidence level. See Tull and Hawkins' Marketing Research, second edition, page 419 for a discussion of sample size adjustment for multinomial data.

Four questions should be raised in class in order to evaluate these findings: (1) Are these registered voters a representative sample of those who will vote in this election: If students respond yes, it is a questionable assertion. (2) How will the undecideds vote? There is no assurance that they will vote in approximately the same proportion as those voters who could and did state a preference of these respondents will parallel those who have made a decision. (4) Are "intention-to-buy" type studies like this one a statistically accurate assessment of demand or merely a quantifiable inference about projected demand? The accuracy of these types of surveys from a historical perspective is questionable.

This section of the case provides the instructor with an excellent opportunity to discuss alternate ways of handling the recurring problem of undecideds and non-respondents and undecideds contained in this survey is not that unusual for this type of survey. Consequently, it is advisable to discuss with the students alternate ways of handling this frequently encountered problem.

Many students will base their evaluation of the findings exclusively upon their interpretation of the data presented in the tables. They should be encouraged in terms of their analytical approach but cautioned about causal inferences concerning simple crosstabulations. None of the simple crosstabulations indicate any overwhelming support for either candidate. These tables have to be evaluated and carefully interpreted in light of the preceding four questions.

Lastly, was Adams correct in concentrating the "promotional blitz" in the precincts that Wagner carried? There is no one correct answer to this question. Some students may argue that more votes could be obtained by concentrating efforts in support precincts rather than campaigning in the weaker ones. Several approaches could be easily defended, but the instructor may wish to question the wisdom of limiting last minute decisive campaigning to a few areas, given the widespread dispersion of the undecideds and the substantial lack of preference for any one candidate. While some precincts may require more effort, there appears to be a need for increasing promotional efforts in the majority of precincts.

4. Identify any additional analysis of the findings which you believe should be made in order to measure the predictability of this study.

The tabulations of responses for Question five, Summary Results of Voter Preference, indicates that approximately 16% of the sample was undecided and almost 5% would not state a preference for either candidate. Consequently, it is necessary to combine the responses of those two groups and see how these grouped respondents evaluate Frank Wagner versus Bill Licking on the dimensions of: (1) success in obtaining community improvements; (2) integrity and honesty; (3) concern for welfare of Hampton residents; and (4) candidates' overall performance as mayor. It would also be insightful to determine if the primary and secondary reasons affecting their vote are significantly different from those of the respondents who stated a preference. Lastly, the questionnaire responses of this group should be crosstabulated by the variable of gender, political affiliation, and precinct in an attempt to define the demographic composition of this group.

It is unfortunate that budgetary constraints did not allow for the inclusion of several filtering questions in the survey. No doubt many of the survey respondents who stated a preference did not vote in this election. The calculation of a filtering index could have been used to select those respondents whose past behavior indicated they would likely vote in this election. Then a separate analysis of the responses of this group could have more precisely predicted the outcome of the election. Without this filtering index and because of the high number of undecideds and non-respondents, a scientific prediction of the outcome of the election was impossible. This is an unfortunate, but common, problem in survey research; therefore, it is wise to acquaint students with the complexities and tradeoffs associated with sampling studies and the need to develop filtering questions.

Postscript: On March 7th, slightly over 60% of the registered voters went to the polls. Frank Wagner lost to Bill Lucking 42% to 58%. A separate analysis of the responses of the undecideds did indicate that this group tended to prefer Lucking over Wagner on the previously discussed dimension.

Another deciding factor was that the Republican precinct workers were successful in getting a lot of their people to the voting stations, whereas the Democrats did not have as effective a transportation network. The survey indicated that Wagner was slightly preferred over Lucking. However, there was a built-in sampling error due to the reduced number of registered voters who actually voted in this campaign. Also, the reduced number of registered voters who actually voted in this campaign. Also, the Republicans launched an intensified promotional campaign during the last three weeks of the campaign and no doubt picked up a high percentage of the undecideds.

Additional Issues For Class Discussion:

1. Should Adams have used the survey data differently than he did? Why or why not?

2. What professional advice should Meyers have given to Adams concerning the interpretation and use of the survey data? Was Meyers professional in his dealings with Adams?

3. Was the survey conducted too late in the campaign and was John Adams at fault for not commissioning a research study in the first few weeks of the campaign?

THE BODINE COMPANY[1]

CASE OBJECTIVES

The objective of this case is to show the problems a small company encounters in introducing a new product into a market that is well established with known product applications. The case focuses on the use of marketing research data in formulating a marketing plan for a new product.

SUMMARY

The Bodine Company, a small manufacturer of electronic products, has developed an eye-mark control device for use in packaging operations, primarily frozen foods. The product was designed and manufactured in response to appeals for help from nearby frozen foods packagers who were experiencing problems with their control mechanisms. In that the eye-mark control was developed in response to market demands, it clearly is superior to competitive brands of which there are several.

Only a handful of eye-mark controls have been sold and all indications are that market entry will be slow. Manufacturers' reps Bodine has used for other products report very little success in selling the eye-mark control (W-20). The problem faced by David Crippen is designing a marketing program that combines awareness and availability. Maintenance or production engineers have to be made aware that there is a control on the market that solves the major problems they have been experiencing on a regular basis. Secondly, some form of distribution scheme must be developed to allow ready availability of the W-20.

Before David Crippen did anything he commissioned a market research study to (1) identify and describe customer-types; and (2) describe customer attitudes toward eye-mark controls in general. The study identified 12 customer targets for replacement sales. Two customer characteristics tend to enhance the potential for a given customer. One is the number of packaging lines in operation. The other is ownership of more than one brand. The most troublesome problem is adjustment of eye sensitivity. The next most troublesome problem is down time. Other problems are difficulties in getting service and parts and the frequent need to change photocells.

QUESTIONS

1. Describe the market for the W-20.

2. Should David Crippen continue to use manufacturers' reps and if so what support should be provided by Bodine?

3. How would you package the W-20?

---

[1].This teaching note is based on materials prepared by H. Robert Dodge.

4.   Design a marketing program for the W-20.

CASE ANALYSIS

1.   Describe the market for the W-20.

     The market for the W-20 is replacement. The OEM market is not promising
for several reasons. Perhaps most important is the fact that packaging
machinery is not readily replaced. Another is that specification of the W-20
is unlikely. Still another is the attitudes of OEM manufacturers when
contacted by Bodine representatives.

     The maintenance engineer is the key purchasing influence. They have a
high degree of tolerance toward control problems of any type. They tend to
live with problems, occasionally buying another brand of control in hopes it
will be better. No brand loyalty was evidenced.

     The most popular brand of control device is Dietz followed by General
Electric, Photoswitch, Farmer Electric and Westinghouse. Explanations for the
multiplicity of brands on the market (15 including Bodine) are possible custom
design and locational convenience in addition to dissatisfaction with a brand.

2.   Should David Crippen continue to use manufacturers' reps and if so what
     support should be provided by Bodine?

     If Bodine does retain the same reps they must supply them with sales
literature, W-20 controls for field demonstrations, and an extra fee for
stocking W-20's. Working against the use of manufacturers' reps is the
relatively low price on the W-20 (reps work on a commission), the fact that
many may not want to stock the W-20 at any price, and the problems of matching
up customer target with manufacturers' rep. For example, it may be
particularly difficult to induce a manufacturer's rep to spend much time
selling a product that will not return substantial financial gain.

3.   How would you package the W-20?

     The W-20 control should be packaged with circuit boards. These circuit
boards should be included with each control. Initially, the W-20 should be
packaged individually.

4.   Design a marketing program for the W-20.

     The proposed marketing program consisted of direct-mail offer for a sixty-
day trial of the W-20 control. Offering a free trial by mail appeared to have
the greatest potential for developing target markets and securing market entry.
At the same time it was the most economical. Manufacturers' reps have shown
little interest in market development and advertising in the appropriate
magazines would seem too general and unlikely to be read by the principal
purchasing influence, the maintenance engineer.

     Direct mail gives Bodine selectiveness plus flexibility in determining the
size of the mailing and thus the amount to be budgeted. Offering a free 60-day
trial period reduces the risk of making a purchasing commitment. Thus, too,

seeing the product in action with its many advantages is a powerful selling inducement. There is also the fact that once installed the customer will be hesitant to dismantle it and send it back to Bodine. The program could be likened to a self-demonstration. Demonstrations are used extensively in industrial marketing.

The theme of the mailing would be as follows: "We would like to introduce you to the W-20 control." The mailing would consist of a folder with sleeves containing a number of inserts. Included in the mailing as inserts would be the following:

1.   A detailed specification sheet with a series of pictures of the W-20 from every angle;

2.   A fact sheet detailing some of the testimonials from maintenance engineers who use the W-20 control;

3.   A sheet giving all the advantages of using the W-20 control;

4.   A sheet outlining an easy-to-understand procedure for setting up the W-20; and

5.   A copy of how to get a W-20 for a free 60-day trial.

The way to get a trial is simple and easy to understand, but respective of Bodine interests. The best way is to have the packager send a purchase order to Bodine with the understanding that no billing will take place for 60 days. The packager could call Bodine's 800 number with the purchase order. Also the 800 number could be used for asking questions and asking for specific installation advice.

THE TRENTEN CORPORATION, MIDCRON DIVISION[1]

CASE OBJECTIVES

The objective of this case is to provide the student with a situation in
which the factors involved with two products in regard to their location in the
product line cycle must be considered before a decision can be reached relative
to marketing strategy for the division. The student has the problem of
identifying the position of the two products as the basis for strategy
development.

SUMMARY

The Midcron Division as part of the Electronics Group for the Trenten
Corporation manufactures a general line of precision electronic switch
products. Total sales of $19.7 million place them 15th among 400 manufacturers
of similar products. The strategic focus for Trenten and Midcron is high tech
and high growth.

In listing advantages and disadvantages, Midcron is positioned in high-
growth markets where competition is fragmented. In addition, their small
market shares make Midcron less subject to notice and subsequent reliatory
action by competitors. Changes in the marketplace favor Midcron.

Among the disadvantages are high-cost assembly fueled by labor costs,
insufficient R & D, and vulnerability to both pricing cuts and new
technological advances.

Two of the products for Midcron are the BA switch and HD switch. Both are
well-established, mature products sold to principally the same market segments.
The major use of the BA switch is in industrial controls while the HD switch is
used principally in automotive and transportation. Total sales of the BA
switch are almost three times that of the HD switch. The BA switch carries a
lower price ($4.90 average) compared to the HD switch ($5.70 average).

The BA and HD switches are sold to both the OEM and replacement markets.
Order size is large for the OEM accounts and small for replacement. The
switches are marketed directly and indirectly through sales reps and electronic
wholesalers.

The major product benefits are dependability and longer product life. In
most instances the OEM customer initiates the sale by asking for a price
quotation. Demand for the switches has been inelastic. Price increases have
had no effect on sales other than increasing the number of dollars involved.

Costs of producing the two switches amount to 70 percent of the sales
dollar. This is higher than other company products because of the labor
involved, the inability to get quantity discounts on materials used and small
batch production. Both switches return a profit before taxes of less than nine

---

[1].This teaching note is based on materials prepared by H. Robert Dodge.

percent or about one-half reported by Midcron as a whole.

QUESTIONS

1. Identify and evaluate the various strategic alternatives for the two switch products.

2. What are the compelling reasons for Midcron moving from labor-intensive to capital-intensive production?

3. Is there a need for Midcron to have more R & D?

CASE ANALYSIS

1. Identify and evaluate the various strategic alternatives for the two switch products.

Do nothing. Keeping the two products in the product line without giving any more sales and advertising support would mean continued decline. The rate of decline would be dependent upon the capabilities of other products to fill the need. Generally, the major market segments for the two switches will be stable or growing slightly in size. The one big risk is that profits from the two switches will fall faster than sales because of the high labor-intensive nature of production.

Raise the price of the products. The two products have shown to be relatively inelastic. Therefore profits should increase with an increase in price. These price increases could off-set production increases, go toward research on product modification, or increase funds for R & D on new products for the same needs.

Discontinue the products. This is not feasible because of the demand of OEM's where the products are part of the existing specification. Also in the replacement market there is a tendency to replace with the same brand. Such action would benefit manufacturing but at a cost of losing out on existing demand.

Product modification. Midcron does not have adequate R & D capabilities. Additionally product modification would add to the price of the product without much chance of increasing returns. The one hope is the modification would restimulate sales. It may be difficult to get capital funding for modification of a poor profit product.

Subcontract the production of the two products. This might be a very viable alternative in that production costs are relatively high for the two switches due to high labor costs. It would also give Midcron flexibility.

Added marketing push. Probably the worst alternative in terms of the nature of both the OEM and replacement markets. For example, added marketing could certainly not increase the rate of replacement.

2. What are the compelling reasons for Midcron moving from labor-intensive to

capital-intensive production?

First and foremost is the fact that Midcron would have more flexibility in pricing in the competitive markets. Another reason is that labor costs will only go up and Midcron is already at a disadvantage. All of the competitors have shifted to machines. Therefore, not having machine-based production is an acknowledged disadvantage.

3. Is there a need for Midcron to have more R & D?

Yes, if they hope to attain the cutting edge of technological change. No, if they can do a good job of marketing products that are copies of the leading products. In other words Midcron must be strong in either R & D or marketing, but not necessarily both.

RAKCO CORPORATION[1]

CASE OBJECTIVES

The student in this case has the task of evaluating a product policy (quality) in actual practice.

SUMMARY

RAKCO, a manufacturer of a wide range of industrial components, has positioned itself as a maker of high-quality, high-performance products. Quality assurance at RAKCO costs $7 million yearly or about two percent of sales. Despite this amount of expenditure, trouble has been experienced with product defects.

Three examples are given to illustrate some of the problems with quality. The problems involved inlet water valves, drain valves, and garage door openers. In each case there was a risk of losing a major customer. With different divisions involved, the procedures followed different patterns.

QUESTIONS

1. Do you feel that RAKCO and its divisions are marketing oriented?

2. Should salespeople be involved in settling quality complaints?

3. Would it be better to have one group or team of quality people handle complaints on quality? State your reasons.

4. Discuss the trade-off of quality with the pricing policy practiced by RAKCO.

5. How would you streamline the procedures used in handling complaints?

CASE ANALYSIS

1. Do you feel that RAKCO and its divisions are marketing oriented?

No, because the complaints of customers such as the noise with drain valves would have been detected before shipping to customer. Whatever quality testing RAKCO does, it is not consumer oriented. It does not subject products to tests based on a customer perspective.

2. Should salespeople be involved in settling quality complaints?

Yes, the salesperson should be the key person in the complaint procedure. The salesperson has the responsibility for sales production which in turn is

---

[1].This teaching note is based on materials prepared by H. Robert Dodge.

seriously affected by complaints. All materials should be funneled through the salesperson. The salesperson should see to it that complaints are solved quickly and fairly.

3. Would it be better to have one group or team of quality people handle all complaints on quality? State your reasons.

    Yes, because in each of the situations, a different sequence is followed. For example, the sales manager attempts to initiate action with the Engineering and Manufacturing Department in regard to the inlet water valves. The follow up was initiated by the quality control manager and quality control engineer.

    However, the quality team should not be reactive. The team should conduct customer-use tests for the products of all the divisions. They should also visit all major customers and discuss quality problems.

4. Discuss the trade-off of quality with the pricing policy practiced by RAKCO.

    RAKCO prices above the market because of the quality and performance built into their products. However, the evidence from these three situations is that customers are not getting the quality they pay extra for. RAKCO can expect customer resistance to present pricing policies.

5. How would you streamline the procedures used in handling complaints?

    If the firm does not utilize a team approach, it would seem important that a uniform procedure be established. The flow should be from sales to quality control with their report forwarded to both sales and manufacturing and design. It is also important that the company gets back to the customer as quickly as possible. Perhaps a committee could be set for each division to consider settlements.

FASHION-PLUS CLOTHING COMPANY[1]

CASE OBJECTIVES

This case presents the student with a pricing strategy problem. The student must integrate fashion marketing strategy, pricing strategy, and cost analysis in reaching a solution. The emphasis in the case is on heuristic problem-solving.

SUMMARY

The Fashion-Plus Clothing Company (FPCC) is considering a new line of high-quality Hawaiian beachware. The shirts are to be marketed through "Dude's Duds," a FPCC sponsored national franchise system and independent retailers. The shirts will bear the Fashion-Plus label in the "Dude's Duds" stores and either the Fashion-Plus label or the retailer's private label in the other stores.

Prices of comparable shirts run from $14 to $17. FPCC knows how much it costs to manufacture and ship shirts. Also known are the sales estimates and associated marketing costs for a skimming-price policy and a penetration price policy.

QUESTIONS

1. In an analysis of costs, determine the variable cost per shirt, the allocation of fixed costs for the new line of Hawaiian shirts, and the total costs per shirt.

2. Compare a penetrating price policy with a skimming price policy for Fashion-Plus.

3. Determine the retail prices for both a penetrating and a skimming price policy.

4. Determine the expected profits and the break-even in dollars and units for both of the pricing policies.

CASE ANALYSIS

1. In an analysis of costs, determine the variable cost per shirt, the allocation of fixed costs for the new line of Hawaiian shirts, and the total cost per shirt.

The direct labor cost per shirt and the transportation cost per shirt must be calculated. All other variable costs are given.

---

[1].This teaching note is based on materials prepared by Jon M. Hawes.

Direct labor cost estimation can be performed in the following manner. The total direct labor cost for last year was $8,000,000. The total number of hours worked was 2,000,000. This means that the average cost per hour was $4 $\frac{\$8,000,000}{2,000,000 \text{ hours}}$ = $4. The new line of shirts requires 20 minutes of direct labor time per shirt. The direct labor variable cost per shirt is $1.33 (1/3 hour x $4).

Determination of the transportation cost per shirt is somewhat more complicated. First, divide the transportation cost for last year ($750,000) by the number of miles for last year (1,250,000). This results in an average cost per mile of $.60. The average cost per mile should now be multiplied by the average number of miles per shipment (225). This results in an average transportation cost of $135 per order. The average order size was 1,000 pounds last year. Thus, the average cost per pound was $.135. This is calculated by dividing the $135 average transportation cost per order by the 1,000 pound average order size. Since each packaged shirt weighs 2 pounds, it would cost about $.27 to deliver a shirt from FPCC to the retailer.

Variable Cost Summary

Cloth	$2.20 per unit
Buttons	.05 per unit
Thread	.05 per unit
Direct labor	1.33 per unit
Transportation	.27 per unit
TOTAL VARIABLE COST	$3.90 per unit

Before a break-even analysis can be conducted, some reasonable means of determining the fixed costs for the new line of shirts must be determined.

A logical way of doing this is to determine the total company fixed costs and then allocate a percentage of this amount to the line of shirts. The fixed cost allocation can be based on sales or labor hours. Labor hours is probably a more accurate basis, as the selling price of the shirt does not influence the fixed cost allocation as would be the case if sales were used as the basis.

Total Company Fixed Cost

Managerial salaries	$1,500,000
Rent and utilities	$1,200,000
Depreciation	$1,300,000
Other overhead	$2,000,000
TOTAL COMPANY FIXED COST	$6,000,000

The new line of shirts will require 20 minutes or 1/3 of an hour of direct labor time for each shirt produced. If a skimming-type pricing policy is used, the Kurt Behrens Market Research Corporation has estimated the sales to be from 110,000 to 130,000 shirts. If 120,000 is used as a most likely estimate, 40,000 labor hours would be required for the production of the shirts (120,000 x 1/3 hour).

If production for the company's other products continues next year at last year's rate, 2,040,000 hours of direct labor time will be required for the production of the company's products. The new line of shirts will account for 1.961% of the company's total direct labor hours (__40,000__).
                                                                   2,040,000

The Kurt Behrens Market Research Corporation has estimated sales to range from 130,000 to 150,000 shirts if a penetration-type pricing policy is used. If 140,000 is used as the most likely estimate, the labor hours required will be 46,666.67 (140,000 x 1/3 hour). Thus, with this pricing strategy, the percentage of direct labor time spent on the new line of shirts would be 2.28% (__46,666.67__).
2,046,666.67

Total company fixed costs were determined to be $6,000,000. If 1.961% is used to allocate the $6,000,000 of company fixed costs when a skimming-type pricing policy is used, the company's fixed cost allocation would be $117,660 ($6,000,000 x 1.961%). If 2.28% is used to allocate the $6,000,000 when a penetration-type pricing policy is employed, the fixed cost allocation would be $136,800 ($6,000,000 x 2.28%). The total fixed cost for the line of new shirts must also include an analysis for the incremental basic marketing costs incurred upon the introduction of the new line. For a skimming-type pricing policy, the incremental basic market cost would be $340,000. Thus for a skimming-type pricing policy, the total fixed cost for the line would be $457,600 ($117,660 + $340,000).

For a penetration-type pricing policy, the incremental basic marketing cost would be $300,000. Thus, in this case, the total fixed cost for the line would be $436,800 ($136,800 + $300,000).

Total Unit Cost Analysis

For a skimming-type pricing policy:

$$TC/unit = FC/unit + VC/unit$$

$$TC/unit = \frac{\$457,600}{120,000 \text{ units}} + \$3.90$$

$$TC \text{ unit} = \$3.8133 + \$3.90$$

$$TC/unit = \$7.7133$$

For a penetration-type pricing policy:

$$TC/unit = FC/unit + VC/unit$$

$$TC/unit = \frac{\$436,800}{140,000 \text{ units}} + \$3.90$$

$$TC/unit = \$3.12 + \$3.90$$

$$TC/unit = \$7.02$$

2. Compare a penetrating price policy with a skimming price policy for Fashion-Plus.

    With a penetrating-price policy, the price of the shirt is set low to stimulate a large volume of sales. A skimming-price policy envisions a small volume of sales but at a higher price. Thus, Fashion-Plus would have to sell more of the shirts at a penetrating price than they would with a skimming price. The appeal with a penetrating-price policy is price which will entail less marketing costs than a skimming-price policy where the appeal would be quality, style, etc.

3. Determine the retail prices for both a penetrating and a skimming price policy.

    The FPCC has two pricing alternatives, according to the facts given in the case. They can employ a skimming or a penetration-type pricing policy. The weighted average retail selling price for similar lines of men's shirts is about $15.53. This is determined from the data presented in the case.

    If FPCC uses a skimming-type pricing policy, the retail selling price would be above $15.53. If FPCC uses a penetration-type pricing policy, the retail selling price would be below $15.53. Assume that $16.00 is selected as the desired retail selling price for a skimming-type pricing policy and $15.00 is selected as the desired retail selling price for a penetration-type pricing policy.

    Since the retailer applies a 40% mark-up on the retail selling price, FPCC would establish $9.60 as their selling price to the retailer for a skimming-type pricing policy and $9.00 for a penetration-type pricing policy. This would probably result in the retail selling price being $16.00 if a skimming-type pricing policy were desired, and $15.00 as the retail selling price if a penetration-type pricing policy were desired.

4. Determine the expected profits and the break-even in dollars and units for both of the pricing policies.

Profit Analysis

For a skimming-type pricing policy:

Profit = Total Revenue - Total Cost

Profit = (SP/unit x units) - (TFC + TVC)

Profit = ($9.60 x 120,000 units) - [$457,600 + ($3.90 x 120,000 units)]

Profit = $1,152,000 - $925,600

Profit = $226,000

For a penetration-type pricing policy:

Profit = Total Revenue - Total Cost

Profit = (SP/unit x units) - (TFC + TVC)

Profit = ($9.00 x 140,000) - [$436,800 + ($3.90 x 140,000 units)]

Profit = $1,260,000 - $982,800

Profit = $277,200

Break-Even Analysis

For a skimming-type pricing policy:

$$\text{BE units} = \frac{FC}{SP/unit - VC/unit}$$

$$\text{BE units} = \frac{\$457,600}{\$9.60 - \$3.90}$$

BE units = 80,280.7 units

BE $ = BE/units x SP/units

BE $ = 80,280.7 units x $9.60

BE $ = $770,823.52

Recap

Skimming		Penetration
	VC/unit	$3.90
$3.90	FC/unit	$3.12
$3.8133	TC/unit	$7.02
$7.7133		
$9.60	FPCC SP/unit	$9.00
$16.00	Retail SP/unit	$15.00
1.961%	% of Company FC allocated to line	2.28%
$117,600	Company FC allocated to line	$136,800
$340,000	Basic marketing cost	$300,000
$457,600	TFC for line	$436,800

80

80,280.7 units	BE units	85,647.056 units
120,000 units	Expected unit sales	140,000 units
$770,694.72	BE $	$770,823.52
$226,400	Expected profit	$277,200

The student should be expected to give a complete analysis of his findings.

FIRST NATIONAL BANK OF FERNWOOD[1]

CASE OBJECTIVES

This case presents a situation in which decision theory can be used in arriving at a course of action involving the pricing of bank services. The emphasis throughout the case is on restoring profitability without a loss in competitiveness.

SUMMARY

The aggressive marketing program called First Deal has in three years increased the customer base by about one third. The First Deal package includes free checking, MasterCard, no or substantially reduced fees on other bank services, and a cash reserve plan. The plan was implemented to remain competitive in the Chicago area but profits have fallen by over 40 percent. The board of directors has initiated action to analyze First Deal customers with a view toward coming up with a revision that increases profits.

The results of the analysis revealed that a substantial proportion of First Deal customers have small checking accounts (average balance of less than $400). Since the bank loses money on these customers, it was decided that something had to be done to remedy the situation. There was a great deal of board sentiment to charging a fee on these accounts. The question remained as to how much of a fee should be affixed. A balance had to be made between additional revenue and loss of customers with the introduction of a fee.

QUESTIONS

1. Do you feel that the First Deal package is a successful marketing program for the bank?

2. Do you agree with Pollard that the major problem rests with those customers having a balance of less than $400?

3. How would you go about solving the problem of which alternative would be best for the bank?

4. Can you propose any alternatives other than a fee structure based on account balance?

CASE ANALYSIS

1. Do you feel that the First Deal package is a successful marketing program for the bank?

First Deal has been successful in terms of adding to the customer base and

---

[1].This teaching note is based on materials prepared by H. Robert Dodge.

use of other bank services. The customer base has increased about one-third and almost all customers use three services and more than half use four services. These increases have been affected despite intensive area competition. The reason that customers keep very little in their respective checking accounts can be explained by the fact that they use checking accounts as convenience mechanisms.

2. Do you agree with Pollard that the major problem rests with those customers having a balance of less than $400?

The accounts below $400 do lose money. With the only difference between accounts being account balance, it would seem that the problem lies with the small account balance. The possible increases with a higher balance are staggering.

3. How would you go about solving the problem of which alternative would be best for the bank?

To compute the gain (loss) from any of three alternatives, several assumptions must be made. For example, the worst case for the first alternative.

Revenue Loss

Checking Account	$ 927	(50% of all customers)
Savings Account	43	(36% who don't have accounts, and 14% who do)
Loans	-0-	(No customers with loans)
MasterCard	779	(23% who don't have card, 27% who do)
Cash Reserve	324	(36% who don't have account, and 14% who do)
Total	$2,073	

Expense Savings

Checking Account	$3,063
Savings Account	22
Loans	-0-
MasterCard	273
Cash Reserve	130
Total	$3,488

Total Revenue	$8,127		
Loss	2,073	$6,054	
$3 (722 customers)		2,166	$8,220
Total Costs	$8,548		
Savings	3,488		
Total Costs (revised)			5,060
New Net Income			$3,160

POSSIBILITIES OF OUTCOMES

Alternative	Worst Case (10%)	Less Than Normal (20%)	Normal Expectation (40%)	More Than Normal (20%)	Optimistic (10%)
$3 below $400	50% 0	40% 5	30% 8	20% 10	15% 20
$2 below $600	45% 4	38% 6	34% 10	30% 15	25% 20
15^ and 10^	50% 2	45% 4	40% 8	35%	25%

BIG SKY OF MONTANA, INC.[1]

CASE OBJECTIVES

This case deals with pricing proposals on ski lifts, rooms, and food services for a forthcoming winter season. The student in making pricing decisions must consider the quantitative and qualitative aspects of consumer, company, and competition. Important to the solution is an analysis of the relationship between price elasticity and contribution margin and profits.

SUMMARY

Big Sky of Montana, Inc., is a medium-sized destination resort that has been in operation for four years. The resort is divided into two main areas. Meadow Village, one of the areas, features lodging, a golf course, and facilities for cross-country skiing in the winter. Mountain Village, the other area, is the center of winter activity.

The facilities, snow conditions, and physical environment of Big Sky compare favorably with other destination resorts in the Rockies. The problem is a lack of awareness that has held down the number of skiers each winter season. The market segments are local day skiers, individual destination skiers, and groups of destination skiers. Individual destination skiers are the largest segment accounting for half of the skier days.

Competition for destination skiers comes from resorts in Colorado, Utah, and Wyoming. Bridger Bowl, a small, no-frills ski resort nearby is the competition for local day skiers.

Without clear pricing objectives, lift rates have been priced higher than local competition but less than destination resorts in other states. Room rates were based on what the market would bear with anticipation of repeat business. The problems with food service hinge around whether to adopt the American plan. Big Sky has been able to realize profits on skiing and lodging, but had a substantial loss on food and beverage service during the last year.

QUESTIONS

1. Prepare an assessment of the company's financial position with respect to operations.

2. Identify potential market segments and their characteristics.

3. Prepare an assessment of the competition.

4. What should the pricing objectives be?

---

[1].This teaching note is based on materials prepared by James Nelson.

5.   Analyze the price elasticity of skiing and lodging.

6.   What should prices be for: (a) ski lifts, (b) rooms, and (c) food
      service.

CASE ANALYSIS

1.   Prepare an assessment of the company's financial position with respect to
      operations.

      Using the information provided in Exhibit 3, ski lift income can be
calculated as shown in Table 1. Knowing that ski lift revenue accounts for 40
percent of all revenue and lodging revenue one-third of total revenue,
approximate income can be determined for the areas of operation and a
breakdown of costs shown for each area. This is shown in Table 2.

      Three basic explanations for the poor performance can be developed:
prices may be too low, cost of sales too high, or operating expenses allocated
unrealistically. Examination of Exhibit 6 in the case tends to eliminate the
first explanation--Big Sky's mean prices lead all competitors. Student
reference to industry sources should indicate that a cost of sales to revenue
ratio of less than 0.6 is reasonably efficient. Thus, the source of the
problem would seem to be the allocation of operating expenses which students
should determine was made on the basis of revenue. Other bases could be
briefly identified such as using costs incurred or contribution margins
generated by the operation. A question that needs to be asked concerns Big
Sky's profitability without the food and beverage operation. Operating
expenses likely will not decline appreciably and a loss would occur, although
there is no information on the composition of operating expenses in the case.

      It is also important to identify an acceptable level of profit for Big
Sky. A before-tax return of 15 to 20 percent on investment will usually
result. However, it should surface that Big Sky has only completed its fourth
year of operation and lower returns may be expected. Other profit mitigating
factors would be the unpredictability of snow conditions and summer operation
profits (which are not a part of the case).

2.   Identify potential market segments and their characteristics.

      There are three consumer segments identified in the case: local day
skiers; individual destination skiers; and group destination skiers
(professional and ski groups). It is important that managerially useful
information be distinguished from merely interesting information. In
particular, the discussion should focus on information that is price relevant.
An attempt to do this is begun in Table 3.

      Income differences in Table 3 are easily explained by income data after
adjusting for inflation. Usage pattern distinctions are also straight-
forward. Destination skiers ski all week and avoid January; locals ski
primarily on weekends throughout the season. Some explanation is required for
the attitudinal differences noted in Table 3. Destination skiers are "on
vacation." They expect to spend money for activities and things for which

they would not at home. Moreover, they see present Big Sky prices as reasonable. All this is in contrast to the local skier who is attitudinally "at home" and things Big Sky prices are high.

Local day skiers likely use a relatively simple decision process. From the case, it appears that local day skiers regularly visit Big Sky each season as a novelty or change of pace from their regular local ski area. By definition, their visit is for only one day at a time so planning for the event is probably minimal. Expected snow and crowd conditions are primary considerations.

The decision process for individual destination skiers is labeled complex. Vacations must be scheduled, air line tickets purchased, and numerous other details arranged before the week-long visit can begin. Likely the decision process involves several competing ski area alternatives which consumers actively compare on numerous decision criteria. In addition to snow and crowd conditions, consumers will consider air fare, lift rates, room rates, ski area reputation, travel convenience, and past experience in making the decision. Outside sources of information both marketer and consumer dominated, will be actively referenced, especially by a first-time purchase.

The decision process for group destination skiers is likely somewhat less involved. Here consumers will make purchase commitments through their group travel arranger. That is, the professional conference chairman, ski club president, or other industrial buyer will make a complex decision while consumers will make a simpler, yes/no decision. Major trip details are the responsibility of the group representative.

Finally, profit potentials of the four segments must be considered. Local day skiers are described as having limited profit potentials for several reasons. Their incomes are low while Big Sky prices are high. In addition, their attitudes toward Big Sky are somewhat cool in general. Relatively few exist as shown by Exhibit 1 in the case. Moreover, they are located some distance from Big Sky with competing areas likely closer. Also, certain local day skiers may be "tied" to closer competing ski areas through a season pass. Finally, local day skiers purchase only a lift ticket, perhaps a lunch, and do not rent a room.

Countering these statements would be the idea that some local day skiers do spend a weekend at Big Sky and need a room and meals. Also, students may validly argue that with only slight increases in marketing effort local day skiers may be induced to visit Big Sky twice a season instead of only once. Or, as another example, they may be induced to spend a night there as a mini-vacation instead of driving long distances home. Both are small changes in behavior that may lead to significant increases in this segment's usage. On balance, however, the long-term profit potential is limited compared to the destination segments.

TABLE 1

LIFT REVENUE BY SKIER CLASS - 1977-78 SEASON

Skier Class	Revenue
Adult All Day All Lift	$ 640,800
Adult All Day Chair	181,800
Adult Half Day	75,200
Child All Day All Lift	68,000
Child All Day Chair	18,500
Child Half Day	7,200
Hotel Passes	280,800
Complimentary	-0-
Adult All Lift Season Pass	30,800
Adult Chair Season Pass	22,275
Child All Lift Season Pass	3,900
Child Chair Season Pass	1,125
Employee All Lift Season Pass	9,100
Employee Chair Season Pass	1,295
TOTAL	$1,340,795

TABLE 2

APPROXIMATE INCOME BY OPERATION - 1977-78 SEASON

	Skiing	Food and Lodging	Beverage
Revenue ($000)	1,341	1,116	895
Cost of Sales			
Merchandise	-0-	-0-	268
Labor	201	177	176
Maintenance	42	58	21
Supplies	20	54	54
Miscellaneous	31	7	5
Operating Expenses	887	741	597
Net Profit (Loss) Before Taxes	160	79	(226)

Several reasons can be cited why this is so. Destination skiers pay for skiing, lodging, and meals. They take ski school lessons. As mentioned earlier, their attitude is one of being "on vacation" and ready to spend. Quantitatively, there are many more destinations than local skiers and they have higher incomes. Finally, students should not lose sight that Big Sky was designed for destination skiers. It contains or should contain everything desired by this segment.

It may be appropriate for the instructor to summarize what has been done so far in the consumer analysis. As discussed and as Table 3 indicated, there exist some very significant differences between local and all destination skiers, with less pronounced differences existing between the three destination segments. Behind all identified differences is the idea of price relevancy. Pricing recommendations based on these differences must be possible or the differences will be managerially inconsequential. On this point, students may successfully argue that Table 3 shows no significant differences between the two group destination skier segments. Quite so, the table entries for both groups are identical. Beyond the entries, however, decision criteria used by the two groups would undoubtedly show differences. For example, professional groups may deduct part or all of certain trip expenses for income taxes, and thus, may be less sensitive to prices. Professional groups would consider the availability of meeting rooms and other professional facilities more important than ski clubs, as another example.

The point is nonetheless well made and the instructor should be prepared to take advantage of it. That is, the instructor must stress that segmentation, to be meaningful, must result in meaningful differences. More subtly, segments and the worth of segmentation depend on the marketing management problem faced by the organization. As an example, pricing segmentation analysis will often lead to different segments than promotion segment analysis. To see this, the instructor can ask if students would still argue for combining the two group destination skier segments into one if promotion instead of pricing strategies were being considered.

Two other conclusions can be made at this point. Other smaller segments likely exist within each of the four identified in Table 3. Not all destination skiers stay at Big Sky, all week, and avoid January dates, for example. More important, while both students and Karen can identify major decision criteria as in this note, they will find it difficult at best to specify the relative importance of each criterion.

A separate and important aspect of the consumer analysis concerns typical expenditures. Table 4 provides details.

TABLE 3

PRICE RELEVANT DIFFERENCES BETWEEN SKIER SEGMENTS

Segment	Approx. 1977 Income	Usage Patterns	Attitudes	Decision Process	Profit Potential
Local day skiers	$16,000	Weekends All season	Recent high prices Skiing is a "home" activity	Simple	Limited
Individual destination skiers	$24,000	All week Avoid January	Prices are reasonable Skiing is a "vacation" activity	Complex	Extensive but travel agent commissions
Group destination skiers (professional)	$24,000	All week Avoid January	Prices are reasonable Skiing is a "vacation" activity	Moderate - Industrial Buyer Behavior	Extensive
Group destination skiers (ski clubs)	$24,000	All week Avoid January	Prices are reasonable Skiing is a "vacation" activity	Moderate - Industrial Buyer Behavior	Extensive

TABLE 4

ESTIMATES OF TYPICAL SKIER EXPENDITURES PER VISIT*

Expenditures	Local Day Skiers	Destination Skiers
Transportation	$25	$250
Lift tickets	12	72
Lodging	0	154
Meals	3	105
Entertainment	3	50
Other	2	34
Total	$45	$665

*Assumes that local day skiers visit for one day and destination skiers visit for seven nights and ski six days.

Student estimates will clearly vary. However, ranges of $40 to $60 and $550 to $800 should include most of their estimates for the two segments. Numbers in Table 5 are rough estimates except for lift tickets and lodging. Lift ticket figures are exact. Lodging can be fairly accurately estimated at $22 per night (Table 2). Transportation charges for destination skiers can be estimated from Exhibit 1 in the case while meal charges can be determined from Exhibit 6.

Both entertainment and other expenditures are casual estimates. Other expenditures include ski lessons, souvenirs, minor equipment purchases, equipment maintenance, and conference fees for the professional group destination skiers.

The main purpose in this analysis is to show the relative proportion of total expenditures per visit accounted for by lift tickets and lodging. For destination skiers, lift tickets are about 11 percent of total expenditures; lodging is about 23 percent. For local day skiers, lift tickets account for about 27 percent of total expenditures but may be perceived by consumers as much more unless they carefully consider automobile expenses.

At this point the instructor might pose the question, "If prices are raised for the 1978-79 season, what will be consumers' perceptions?" The answer, of course, depends on consumer segment. Local day skiers will perceive a $2 lift ticket increase, for example, far differently than destination skiers. Different incomes, attitudes, and reference to Weber's Law all point to this conclusion.

3.   Prepare an assessment of the competition.

A good approach here is to orient the discussion about a comparison of Big Sky's and competing destination areas' product and price mixes. Students should be able to determine that these ski areas are older, well-established resorts with national reputations. They have more lifts (Exhibit 2 in the case) and more skiers. Likely they are more crowded, given Karen's statement. Because of greater experience, competing destination areas perhaps have "smoother" operations. There are likely fewer pleasant and unpleasant surprises for skiers, more well-defined organizational activities and jobs, and more routinized decision making.

The pricing comparison is less distinct. Lift prices for the five competing destination areas are generally higher, averaging $12.80 (Exhibit 2) compared to Big Sky's $12.00. Moreover, these lift prices are expected to rise $1 or $2 next year. Lodging rates are generally competitive with Big Sky's rates as shown in Table 5.

Referring to Table 5, competing area rates are again determined from Exhibit 2 in the case while Big Sky rates come from Exhibit 4. The range of rates for Big Sky is based on low and high season minimums in Exhibit 4 for the occupancies shown in Table 5.

TABLE 5

PER PERSON LODGING RATE COMPARISON

		Per Person Room Rates		
Accommodation Type	Occupancy	Competing Area Average	Big Sky Range	Big Sky Accommodation
Lodge double	2	$21.60	$21-25	Huntley Lodge (Standard)
Two-bedroom Condominium	4	$22.78	$20-23	Stillwater Condo (bedroom with loft)
			$23-25	Deer Lodge Condo (two bedrooms)
Three-bedroom Condominium	6	$18.93	$18-20	Deer Lodge Condo (three bedrooms)

4. What should the pricing objectives be?

There are no pricing objectives for Big Sky operations. Students should spend time on this topic, concluding that Karen's job would be easier if corporate pricing expectations were stated formally. From the case, it would appear that three objectives could be developed:

   (1) Earn an acceptable return on investment (as mentioned in the preceding paragraph);

   (2) Level demand fluctuations by increasing January usage; and

   (3) Provide special pricing to the local market to moderate "local resentment concerning Big Sky's lift rate policy."

Students should recognize that recommendations to Big Sky should address at least these three objectives.

5.   Analyze the price elasticity of skiing and lodging.

An analysis of price elasticities for skiing and lodging is shown in Table 6. All values must be calculated from data presented in Exhibits 3, 4, and 5. Straight-forward manipulations of data in Exhibit 3 yield the skiing values. However, it is necessary to use average revenues and usage rather than totals for the elasticity calculation because of the different operating season lengths. Skiing price elasticity is calculated by $e = \dfrac{\Delta Q}{Q} / \dfrac{\Delta P}{P}$ or [(988 - 910)/910] divided by [($9.97 - $8.85)/$8.85] which equals +.68.

TABLE 6

SKIING AND LODGING PRICE ELASTICITY DATA

	Total Revenue	Total Usage*	Operating Days	Average Revenue	Average Usage*	Price Elasticity
Skiing						
1977-78	1,340,795	134,430	136	$ 9.97	988	+.68
1976-77	983,930	111,080	122	8.85	910	
Lodging						
1977-78	1,116,000	49,550	124	22.52	399	-.73
1976-77	?	59,225	122	19.00 (est.)	488	-.98

*Usage is measured in skier days for skiing, person nights for lodging.

That the elasticity coefficient is positive is quite surprising. Students should be urged to interpret this result. Possible explanations are Big Sky's relative infancy and a prestige demand curve.

Lodging calculations are more involved and require Exhibits 4 and 5 in the case plus knowledge that total lodging revenue is approximately $1,116,000 for 1977-78. From Exhibit 5, students can calculate total lodging usage for the 1977-78 season. Again, it is appropriate to use average usage and revenue in the elasticity calculation because of the difference in operating days between the two seasons.

Calculations for the 1976-77 season are more difficult and require the student to estimate average lodging revenue. Capable undergraduate and graduate students may perform the estimation unaided. For other students, instructors may want to provide the information that total lodging revenue was $1,066,000 for the 1976-77 season when assigning the case. The estimation comes from Exhibit 4 in the case. Using both low and high season rates, students can calculate average ranges for the two seasons and conclude lodging prices went up approximately $11 to $15. Using say, $13 as the average increase and $65 as the average 1976-77 room rate, average revenues increased $13/$65 or 20 percent for the 1977-78 season. Thus, average room revenue for 1976-77 season is $22.08/1.2 or $19 (rounded).

Average lodging usage is easily calculated with no estimation from Exhibit 5 in the case. Lodging price elasticity is calculated by $e = \frac{\Delta Q}{Q} / \frac{\Delta P}{P}$ or [(399-488)/488] divided by [($22.52 - 19.00)/$19.00] which equals -.98.

As another comment on price elasticities, students will note the interrelatedness of Karen's decision. That is, prices must be developed for three complementary products in the product mix. Students will frequently argue on both quantitative and qualitative bases that one or two product lines (or items) be given away as "loss leaders" to maximize overall profit for the firm. Because a complete discussion requires consumer and competitive in addition to company considerations, the matter is deferred until later in this note.

For now, it is important to note that a primary concept to use in this analysis is price cross elasticity of demand. However, because prices for both lodging and skiing increased in the 1977-78 season, price cross elasticities are impossible to calculate.

In summary, the magnitude of the lodging price elasticity coefficient at -.98 which is close to unit elasticity. Because student estimates will differ, a range of -1.5 to -0.5 for this coefficient can be expected. Because of varying estimates, natural growth of the infant operation, weather differences, and inflation, price elasticity calculations for the two years' operations will be approximate at best. Thus, elasticity coefficients should be used as guides in pricing and not absolute determinants of strategy. The inelastic coefficient for lodging resulted in only a slight lodging revenue increase when prices were increased for 1977-78. However contribution margins show a significant increase as shown below:

	1977-78 Season	1976-77 Season
Total Lodging Revenue ($000)	1,116	1,066
Total Variable Cost ($000)	296	354
Contribution Margin ($000)	820	712

Data for 1977-78 come from Table 2. Revenue for 1976-77 is determined by multiplying $18.00 times 59,225 person nights usage (Exhibit 5 in the case). Total variable costs for 1976-77 are determined by multiplying the average variable cost for 1977-78 ($5.97) times 59,225 person nights.

Students should also determine at what relative percentage of capacity the skiing and lodging operations are currently operating. Using 130 days as a common season for skiing and lodging, skiing capacity is 4,000 skiers per day times 130 days or 520,000 skier days. Lodging capacity is exactly half-- 2,000 beds times 130 days or 260,000 person nights. Percentages of capacity are 134,430/520,000 or 25.9 percent and 49,550/260,000 or 19.1 percent for skiing and lodging, respectively.

A last company analysis concerns Karen's reaction to the American Plan proposal. Students should recognize there is limited or no data to support or deny the proposal and that adoption of the plan now for all destination skiers is not prudent. At best, the American Plan may only be tried on selected groups of group destination skiers who can be informed before arriving and whose reaction can be carefully measured. In addition to gaining some experience with the American Plan, this trial period will allow experimentation with pricing, and leases to expire for independent restaurants. This last condition is especially important because requiring destination skiers to participate in the plan next year will cause dissatisfaction, given prices currently charged by these restaurants (Exhibit 6).

6. What should prices be for: (a) ski lifts, (b) rooms, and (c) food service?

Increase average lift revenue $2.00. Support for this recommendation can be found in the company, consumer, and competitive analyses. From the elasticity analysis, one would expect usage to change little with the increased prices. Students' pro forma income statements for skiing should show a revenue increase of about 20 percent with net profit before taxes more than doubling, assuming the cost structure is relatively constant. From the consumer analysis, a price increase is supported by showing the small portion of a destination skier's total expenses accounted for by ski lift tickets. Students may also discuss relevant attitudes, including a price/quality relationship that may exist in consumers' minds with respect to choosing a destination area. Local day skiers will object to the price increase, however, and some strategic consideration must be given to this segment. Finally, the competitive analysis easily supports this price increase. Even with the increase, Big Sky's lift prices likely will be somewhat lower still than next year's competing prices.

Increase average lodging revenue 5 percent. Supporting this recommendation are analyses showing lodging demand much more price sensitive than skiing, competitive lodging rates slightly lower than Big Sky's, and lodging accounting for a large proportion of the typical destination skier's expenditures. It is, in fact, the largest such expenditure controlled by Big Sky. Students may also note that lodging is currently operating at a lower percent of capacity than skiing.

Students will infrequently argue for "loss leading" the skiing and making higher profits on lodging. Such a policy is supported by area capacity, local skier, and U.S. Forest Service considerations. Countering are the price elasticity, competitive, destination skier, and profit considerations as raised in this note.

On the other hand, students may take an opposite position and argue for low lodging and higher skiing rates and cite similar support. In both instances, students are assuming something about consumer decision criteria not evident in the case. This forms the basis for the following recommendation.

1. Undertake some formal consumer research in the 1978-79 season to determine what features destination skiers consider important in selecting Big Sky from competing areas. If time permits, students should identify an appropriate research design.

2. Try the American Plan on several groups of group-destination skiers (both professional and ski clubs). During the trials, it will be important to use different plans and prices and to measure both consumer and management reaction. Again, if time permits, students should develop specific research plans.

3. Make a special pricing and promotion plan to satisfy local day skiers. Perhaps better than the present $9.00 chair lift only ticket would be couponing for skiing or lodging price reductions in January. Montana newspapers and nearby ski shops could both be used to distribute coupons. It is important that the activity be identified as for local skiers and that their reactions to it be measured.

4. Karen should be urged to identify specific pricing objectives as in this note and discuss them with top management in Michigan. Such goals would provide direction, a measure of performance and control, and serve as an excellent communications vehicle in the decentralized operation.

5. Big Sky may attempt to bargain with several smaller destination skier groups to move them to January from the more crowded periods. A special price incentive may be used. The point to be made is that Big Sky has some bargaining power that can reasonably be exploited.

A Final Note

A temporary $1.00 increase was placed for all day tickets during the Christmas holidays and the chair-only tickets will be dropped for the season. While it is impossible to determine the exact effect of these changes, an estimate of average skiing revenue rising $.50 to $.75 seemed reasonable.

Lodging prices were simplified to a single price per room basis, regardless of season and occupancy, and reduced approximately 5 percent. Again, the effect is impossible to determine but expected demand for lodging seemed to increase 5-8 percent.

Finally, a promotion tie-in with the air carriers was undertaken to reduce significantly air fares charged to destination skiers. The net effect of these pricing changes was to make it cheaper for skiers to visit Big Sky. That, historically, Big Sky prices have not appeared to be a significant dimension in the consumer decision process has not convinced management to act otherwise. A major concern of management in the price setting process was the local reaction to price changes. With the rather minimum increases in 1978-79, such reaction was to be quite favorable. Yet, because of heavy skier demand during the holidays (not described in the case), management expects average skiing revenues to increase somewhat more than the $.75 estimated above. And, based on 1978-79 results, further price increases may be needed for the 1979-80 season.

Thus, management is anticipating a skiing revenue increase of the order recommended but over a two-year period. This idea of a gradual change instead of an immediate 20 percent revenue increase is important for students to grasp. No evidence of the need for dramatic changes can be found in the case. Indeed, the 1977-78 lodging usage experience and skiing income figures point otherwise.

FRANK W. HORNER Ltd.[1]

CASE OBJECTIVES

1. The case provides an opportunity to formulate an advertising and promotion plan and to evaluate a current plan.

2. The case enables the student to evaluate the affects of culture on advertising decisions.

3. Students are exposed to media selection, message content and advertising budget decisions.

4. The case may be useful in giving the students an opportunity to evaluate preliminary technical and market research procedures.

SUMMARY

Frank w. Horner Ltd. of Montreal distributes a variety of ethical and over-the-counter (OTC) pharmaceutical products. The company's products are distributed to 4000 pharmacies across Canada through a sales force of sixty-five persons. In April 1978, management was planning the 1978-79 communication strategy for the Fevertest. This product consisted of a thin plastic strip which, when applied to the forehead, indicated whether or not an individual had a fever. The initial promotional campaign for Fevertest between November 1977 and the end of March 1978 was Horner's first consumer-type promotion. Management was wondering whether they could improve sales by investing in television advertising, an approach which had not previously been used.

QUESTIONS

1. Discuss the Fevertest's competitive environment.

2. Is television advertising an effective way to promote the Fevertest?

3. Should Horner distribute the Fevertest to supermarkets?

4. How much should Horner spend on their 1978-79 media campaign and how much should it be allocated?

5. What copy themes for the Fevertest should be highlighted?

1This teaching note was prepared by John A.Quelch of The Harvard Business School. Copyright c 1978 by The University of Western Ontario. Reproduced by permission.

CASE ANALYSIS

1. Discuss the Fevertest's competitive environment.

    Consumer research indicated that 84 percent of consumers follow up an
    indication of fever on the Fevertest with a thermometer reading. The
    Fevertest supplements the thermometer and does not serve as a replacement.
    Thus, the competitive threat to the Fevertest is from other fever
    indicators and not glass thermometers.

    In early 1978, company estimates indicated that the Fevertest held 95
    percent of the Canadian fever indicator market. Only one direct
    competitor, Stik Temp, was known to have been distributed in Canada.
    Similar products to the Fevertest were on sale in the United States,
    however, including Clinitemp, Fever Tester and Fever Meter. Management
    believed that many of these products would eventually be distributed in
    Canada.

    Horner should recognize the potential competitive threats and take steps
    to head-off successful introductions of other fever indicators. The
    Fevertest had a great advantage in Canada because they were the first
    fever indicator on the market. They have an excellent opportunity to
    maximize the awareness of the Fevertest so that consumers automatically
    think of the name when they consider the concept of a fever indicator.
    High product awareness will help differentiate the Fevertest from the
    other inferior fever testers. It is very easy for consumers to mistake
    the "Fever Tester" with Horner's "Fevertest" product. Without high brand
    awareness Horner's advertising campaign will benefit the entire product
    class instead of only the Fevertest. Thus, Horner can take advantage of
    its early entrance into the market by quickly implementing a large
    promotional push that will establish the Fevertest as the only fever
    indicator that comes to a consumer's mind when they consider a purchase.

2. Is television advertising an effective way to promote the Fevertest?

    Most students will probably recommend that Horner undertake television
    advertising to sell the Fevertest. The Vancouver advertising test seems
    to indicate that TV advertising significantly increased Fevertest sales.
    The sales increased from an average of 40 cases a week before the
    advertising to 144 cases during the eight week period following the three
    week advertising period. These incremental sales result in a profit of
    $26,957 [(Additional Case Sales/Week X Margin/Case X# Weeks) (144-40) X
    15.98 X 8 = $26,957] versus the $17,650 cost of advertising. Also,
    awareness in Vancouver was significantly higher than in Calgary where no
    commercials were shown.

    We believe that the Vancouver television advertising campaign offers
    convincing but not conclusive evidence that television ads should be used
    to promote the Fevertest. The major problem is the lack of control in the
    test market. For example, a flue epidemic in the Vancouver area may have
    occurred during the test period that could have accounted for part or all
    of the increased sales. The test was run in the middle of winter when the

use of the Fevertest could be expected to be at its highest levels of the year. National sales levels tended to be higher during the test period which may indicate that sales would have increased even without the advertising. Also, the effectiveness of the commercial itself was not evaluated. Other problems are the company's lack of experience in television advertising and the possibility that television advertising would benefit similarly named competitive products as much as Fevertest.

3. Should Horner distribute the Fevertest to supermarkets?

There are many advantages to distributing the Fevertest to supermarkets. These outlets would probably be eager to handle the fever indicator because of the opportunity for high margins per square foot of selling space. With the trend toward large "superstores" more and more items that were formerly sold exclusively at pharmacies are being carried by food retailers. The most obvious advantage, of course, is that management expects sales to be up to three times higher with supermarket distribution. The primary target market, mothers of young children, often shop in supermarkets and will be exposed to the Fevertest on a regular basis if it is sold in food stores. Also, potential competition could be forestalled before they have a chance to move into supermarkets.

This broad distribution strategy is not without its risks however. There may be a negative effect on Horner's reputation despite the increased acceptance of selling items in supermarkets that were formerly only sold through drug stores. Pharmacies may withdraw support from Fevertest, particularly if supermarkets sell the product at a lower rate. Finally, the Fevertest may lose its credibility if Horner cannot ensure that it is not sold as a novelty or gimmick item. Loss of marketing control may be a problem with a broad distribution strategy.

4. How much should Horner spend on their 1978-79 media campaign and how should it be allocated?

Students will differ significantly in their recommendations about advertising expenditures and media selection. Regardless of their conclusions, students should go through the marketing communication decision model presented in the text. Basically, we have used the task approach presented in the text to formulate our program.

Management's estimate of sales of 500,000 units with sales restricted to pharmacies and 1,500,000 units if distribution is broadened appear to be very subjective in light of past sales experience. Actual sales of only 317,000 units in a five-month winter period and sales of 1,000,000 units in France (a market twice the size of Canada) in a one yaer period indicate that sales in the 1978-79 year will fall somewhere between management's high and low estimates. We will assume supermarket distribution and the implementation of a television advertising campaign. Given these assumptions a sales objective of one million units or $1,350,000 is probably reasonable. This sales level leaves $665,833 for advertising and profits [Profit Margin in %/Case X $ Sales = 15.98/32.40 X $1,350,000 = $665,833]. Assuming a twenty percent rate of return on sales is desired [.2 X $1,350,000 = $270,000] then $395,833 is available for advertising. It is difficult to estimate, but this amount should be enough to achieve the desired sales levels.

With the initial introduction completed, relative emphasis should probably be placed on gaining mass exposure and awareness for the Fevertest. Thus, television advertising should be utilized within the constraints of the budget. Television advertising may be tested further to determine its affectiveness. Different levels of advertising may be tried simultaneously in several different markets to determine an optimal amount to meet company objectives. For example, flights of only ten days or two weeks may be more cost effective than three or four week flights. Point of purchase and, to a lesser extent than previously, consumer magazine advertising should also be utilized. Television advertisements and point of purchase displays accounted for 89% of consumers source of Fevertest information in Vancouver.

Maximizing advertising reach is probably advantageous with a low priced product and a broad distribution strategy. One possible budget allocation is presented below.

$358,833 Total $ available for advertising
 262,395 Seven weeks of national television advertising (7 X $37,485)
 133,438
  59,000 Point of purchase displays
  83,438
  20,000 Cooperative advertising
  63,438
  63,438 Consumer magazine advertising
 000,000

As stated earlier, tests should be run to determine the most efficient use of the seven available weeks of national television advertising. One alternative may be one three-week flight followed by two two-week flights. Also, different locations may need different amounts of advertising to reach an awareness level of, say, 70%.

We allocated $50,000 to point of purchase displays to continue last year's program and to purchase the new motorized counter displays. Pharmacies can be given these displays to help offset their possible discontent about competing with supermarket distribution of the Fevertest and it will help ensure their continued support for the product. Cooperative advertising will help pharmacy relations and help maintain their marketing support. It also stretches Horner's advertising dollars.

We allocated the rest of the advertising funds ($63,438) to consumer magazine ads and miscellaneous expenditures. The Vancouver tests revealed that, with television advertising, magazine ads added very little to consumer awareness level of the Fevertest. If awareness can be gained by television advertisements we believe that making the product readily available with broad distribution and supported by point of purchase displays will be the test way to maximize sales. Thus, magazine advertisements are given less emphasis.

5. <u>What copy themes for the Fevertest should be highlighted</u>?

Ease of use is probably the Fevertest's greatest selling point.
Television ads and a sample Fevertest at many of the point of purchase
locations can best highlight this advantage. The unbreakable nature of
the product will also be noted by consumers at point of purchase.

Consumers should be reassured about the accuracy of the Fevertest. This
is probably the biggest disadvantage of the product in the eyes of the
consumers. They should be aware that the Fevertest accurately indicates
the presence of a fever and is superior to other similar fever indicators.

Finally, the low price and reusable nature of the Fevertest should be made
explicit. Consumers have had the misconception that the Fevertest was
disposable.

MORTON SALT[1]

CASE OBJECTIVES

This case is designed to provide students with experience in evaluating the marketing communications efforts of a well-established firm offering essentially a parity product.

SUMMARY

Morton Salt's generating brand preference in a parity market has been the result largely of its ability to provide innovations whenever changes have occurred in the marketplace. Innovative packaging and brand promotion allowed it to differentiate itself initially. However, when its premium price produced some consumer resistance, the addition of iodine provided a product innovation.

Similarly, when declining usage and shifting eating patterns were evidenced in the marketplace, Morton used a repositioning strategy and introduced a series of innovative line extensions. Most recently, as medical concerns over the use of salt were evidenced, Morton's innovative new product development program, coupled with an aggressive advertising and sales promotion program, allowed Morton to continue its domination of the market.

QUESTIONS

1. What basic problems face Morton Salt in marketing regular table salt?

2. Can consumer sales for regular table salt be increased substantially through advertising?

3. Should the sales promotion approach used by Morton for regular table salt in the past few years be continued?

4. Suggest some sales promotion ideas that might help Morton increase sales of regular table salt.

5. Since no link between salt used and diseases has actually been proved, should Morton challenge medical and governmental authorities and counter criticisms in its advertising for regular table salt?

6. What is Morton's best future course for marketing regular table salt?

7. Is it possible to target at markets other than consumers to expand potential sales?

8. Can Morton capitalize on the trend toward unbranded consumer package goods?

---

[1]. This case was prepared by Charles H. Patti, Associate Professor of Marketing, and Debra Low, Faculty Associate, Arizona State University. Used with permission.

CASE ANALYSIS

1. What basic problems face Morton Salt in marketing regular table salt?

    Morton Salt faces two basic problems in marketing regular table salt:

    Regular table salt is a product in the maturity stage of the product life cycle and, as such, suffers the problems of any mature product. It is no different from, and offers no advantages over, competitive products. There is no particular claim Morton can make in its advertising to consumers other than its brand name, which is admittedly stronger and better known than any competitor's.

    Regular table salt is the target of growing concern of medical and governmental authorities, due to the hypothesized link between salt use and certain diseases. The problem is compounded by the increased awareness of health and fitness among Americans. The success of products that substitute for salt attests to the seriousness of the problem. Morton is marketing a product, regular table salt, that people are increasingly reluctant to use and against which consumers are being warned more and more every day.

2. Can consumer sales for regular table salt be increased substantially through advertising?

    Probably not, since no advantage can be claimed and since consumers are showing increased concern over salt use. In addition, substitute products are growing in popularity.

    The only reasonable possibility for increased sales through advertising is a sales promotion approach, such as Morton has been using. Consumers must be given some extra reason to purchase--such as premiums, contests, or new product uses.

3. Should the sales promotion approach used by Morton for regular table salt in the past few years be continued?

    Yes. Sales promotion is often the only successful strategy for a mature product. It gives consumers an extra reason to purchase, without which Morton regular table salt sales probably will not increase.

4. Suggest some sales promotion ideas that might help Morton increase sales of regular table salt.

    Ideas that promote a new, nonconsumption use of regular table salt are best, since such uses avoid medical criticism. Salt sculpture, for example, was a very successful idea for Morton.

    Ideas that trade on the strength of the Morton brand name and its history may be successful. They may not, however, be perceived by consumers as distinct from past promotions, such as the special packages or porcelain mugs.

Ideas that promote heavier salt consumption should be avoided, since this may invite direct criticism of Morton by medical and/or government authorities.

5. Since no link between salt use and diseases has actually been <u>proved</u>, should Morton challenge medical and governmental authorities and counter criticisms in its advertising for regular table salt?

No. This course would be an open invitation for public criticism. Growing consumer interest in health and fitness indicates that people probably endorse the idea of less salt use. Whether or not the link between salt use and disease is true, consumer <u>perception</u> of its truth should be the basis for future Morton actions (as it has been in the past, as evidenced by introductions of Salt Substitute and Lite Salt).

6. What is Morton's best future course for marketing regular table salt?

Morton could continue its sales promotion approach, particularly promoting new uses for salt. This is probably the only method of sustaining and increasing sales.

Morton could cut back advertising and sales promotion to minimal levels and use regular table salt as a "cash cow," to support other products in its line of new products. As Morton's president noted, while regular table salt is only 5 percent of tonnage sales, it represents 35 percent of dollar sales. This is often a solution for companies with well-known products that produce good revenues but do not have much hope for growth.

7. Is it possible to target at markets other than consumers to expand potential sales?

Yes, trade promotions/advertising offers a potential vehicle. Co-op advertising, point-of-purchase displays, delayed billing, and quantity discounts should be examined.

Additionally, institutional sales should be pursued more aggressively (such as schools, hospitals, prisons, and so on). Perhaps packaging in the premeasured quantities common to institutional food preparation would provide an innovative edge.

8. Can Morton capitalize on the trend toward unbranded consumer package goods?

Yes, Morton could consider the economies of supplying store brand products, potentially reducing marketing expenditures and yet expanding overall volume. The obvious tradeoff to be considered here concerns the detriment to Morton's long-established brand image.

TEXAS GRAPE GROWERS ASSOCIATION[1]

CASE OBJECTIVES

1. To demonstrate the special problems a new competitor faces in gaining a foothold in an established market.

2. To illustrate the importance of target market definition in developing a strategy for a new product.

3. To illustrate how an expansion of the original target market can be integrated into the long-term planning process.

SUMMARY

   This case examines the problems faced by a relatively small group of Texas grape growers in developing a strategy for their product. Due to the dominance of New York and California in the domestic wine industry, the Texas growers have adopted a strategy of first marketing their wines at the local level, with a gradual expansion into the national market. The case allows the student to consider how priorities can be set in the selection of target markets.

QUESTIONS

1. Evaluate the TGGA's decision to concentrate initially on the Texas market.

2. How should the TGGA proceed in expanding beyond its initial Texas market?

3. What should the TGGA's strategy be for expansion into other markets?

CASE ANALYSIS

1. Evaluate the TGGA's decision to concentrate initially on the Texas market.

   The decision of the TGGA to initially focus on the Texas market seems to be a sound one:
   -the market for wine in Texas has grown faster than the national rate (which itself has seen a large amount of growth):
   -problems due to the lack of a brand image is likely to be diminished, due to the "home state" nature of the product;
   -limited resources dictate that TGGA concentrate their efforts on the market(s) with the most potential. The danger of spreading resources too thin arises if too broad a market is defined.

2. How should the TGGA proceed in expanding beyond its initial Texas market?

   Future plans should include expansion outside of the Texas market. By assessing the wine-drinking population as a whole, the TGGA can decide on the most effective route of expansion. The demographic information provided in the case demonstrates that wine consumption is greater among younger, better-

---

   [1]. This case was prepared by Ronald J. Faber and Tom O'Guinn.

educated and wealthier segments of the population. Also, women seemed to form a strong market for wine products. An analysis of psychographics/lifestyle characteristics may be appropriate in order to ascertain which segments of the population are likely to be early innovators, or otherwise accepting of a new and/or unproven wine product.

3.   What should the TGGA's strategy be for expansion into other markets?

The TGGA should continue to make use of information as it proceeds with its expansion. Marketing research can play a pivotal role in developing a strategy for the wine. Information regarding awareness, knowledge and attitudes towards the product should be gathered on a regular basis as the expansion proceeds in order to discover problem areas.

The TGGA has gotten off to a good start in obtaining information about the U.S. wine market in general, and the Texas market in particular. Now information is needed about the wine drinking patterns in other, more specific areas of the country.

The overall strategy for the company should include an emphasis on the communication of its product's availability and quality both to distributors and to consumers. At the present time, the TGGA's largest obstacles are those centering on a lack of knowledge and credibility regarding their product.

QUICK MEAL FOOD SYSTEMS INC.[1]

CASE OBJECTIVES

This case illustrates the problem of determining a budget and operating plans for the first year of operation in a new business. The objective of the case is to illustrate how such plans should be constructed based on a careful analysis of the marketing research data provided. Several alternative plans can be generated based on sales forecasts and required capital decisions. The objective is to show that, before considering a new venture, careful market study must be conducted. Students should examine the available data and collect some additional data, such as operating costs (for a fast-food restaurant) and estimates of the costs of promotional activities. This data can be obtained from fast-food outlets located in their respective areas.

SUMMARY

The QM company is actually Hardee's chain. Students who trace the Fortune article mentioned in the case would no doubt discover this fact. The case deals with the rapid growth strategy embarked upon by Hardee's. However, since most students will experience such strategic goals only later in their careers, the case focuses on the opening of one restaurant as a specific example of such a strategy.

The setting is a campus town where Hardee's is about to open a new restaurant. Students are the main target market, and the case supplies some basic information about their eating preferences, media habits, and specific features (hours of operation, and so forth). Students are more likely to face such problems during the first years of their careers.

The main problem, therefore, is Hardee's pursuit of growth strategy which brings about a rush for opening new outlets. The problems facing the manager of this new store are described, along with the lack of good quality data for making decisions.

Some secondary problems include:

a. What kind of promotional strategy should be used? What are the objectives? Why?

b. In addition to the data available, what kinds of marketing research data is needed? Can the manager target his promotion without this data?

c. How should the first year's operating budget be distributed? What are the parameters needed for making budget decisions, a sales forecast, and expense and profit forecasts.

QUESTIONS

1. Develop a media campaign for the new store. Don't forget sales promotion and publicity stints.

2. How much would you recommend be spent on an advertising campaign? As a guideline, use an estimate for revenues generated.

3. What kinds of other promotional materials would you recommend? Can you consider cooperation with student groups, clubs, and so forth?

4. Develop a forecast of demand for the new restaurant based on the data available. What would the first year's sales be?

5. What information, other than that supplied by the survey, would you ideally want to have? How much would you be willing to spend on obtaining it?

6. What secondary sources (available in your library) would you use to gather additional information about this new market opportunity?

7. Can you think of primary sources for data collection (that is, local restaurants, writing to Hardee's (QM), and so forth)?

CASE ANALYSIS Several facts are pertinent to the primary problem

a. The chain has embarked on a quick-growth strategy. Exhibits 1-3 provide data as to the financial strength of the company, its distribution network, modes of operations, and past acquisition's experience.

b. No data are given to support the opening of this new store at this time at this particular location. The data available to the manager does not seem to justify opening this new store.

c. The survey of demand was not done competently--leading to yet more useless data. Much of the data needed was not collected.

Obviously the fact that the data in the case is insufficient dictates two courses of action:

a. If possible, the store shouldn't be opened.

b. If it cannot be closed, the manager must be able to have strategy and budget a promotional campaign. It must first be decided what the primary targets are. This cannot be done based on the data about the townspeople (it is too vague). The data about the students lack specific questions about the need for the additional outlets, the frequency of eating out, the amount spent on meals outside the home, dorm, and so forth. A complete strategy is needed.

It is expected that most students will ignore the first course of action. However, there is nothing in the case which would be an argument against this course of action. Most students recommend the second course of action, yet neglect to ask the crucial question: What is the strategy for this store? Most students propose one form or another of the following: Embark on additional data collection which will lead to additional and better information about the store's feasible strategies. Pricing, promotional campaigns, and additional information are called for. The students propose different campaigns, strategies, and other direct forms of promotional activities to a student population. Some also revise strategies for other local residents. However, few stop to ask: What is the overall strategy for the store?

DISCUSSION

This case affirms the General Foods Hypothesis: "Good planning is more important than good execution and control." This case shows how haphazard location study leads to opening an outlet in the wrong place. No one stops to ask the real questions: Is there a need, a target? Is there a strategy? Rather the focus is on promotional/marketing research data, both of which are essentially side issues. Most students tend to resolve these problems rather than ask whether this store should operate at all. The problem is reading between the lines to find the fundamental issue rather than be sidetracked by irrelevant data, which further aggravates incorrect initial decisions.

The case can also enhance discussion of:

a. Strategic decisions.

b. Data requirements (that is, the importance of planning for data collection).

c. The importance of setting objectives for promotion campaigns.

1.1This case was prepared by Michael V. Laric, University of Connecticut, with the intention of providing a basis for class discussion rather than illustrating either effective or ineffective management of a business situation. Reprinted with permission from Application of Decision Sciences in Organizations: A Case Approach by Joseph C. Latona and K. Mark Weaver with the cooperation of the Decision Sciences Institute (formerly The American Institute for Decision Sciences).

TOMMY'S TOYS AND THINGS[1]

CASE OBJECTIVES

This case is designed to assist the student in developing an awareness of general legal/regulatory concerns and an understanding of selected practice restrictions enforced by the FTC affecting retail merchants. The case can also be used to stimulate class discussion on the effect of governmental controls, regulatory cost factors, advertising as public policy, and attorney-retailer interactions.

SUMMARY

Tommy's Toys and Things has received a letter of complaint from the Federal Trade Commission requiring immediate action. Tommy Tomison, CEO of Tommy's Toys and Things, felt certain that the complaint resulted from a recent series of advertisements. Tommy must decide whether or not the ads constitute an unfair or deceptive trade practice and what action to take.

QUESTIONS

1. How should Tommy determine whether or not the advertisements in the series are in probable violation of the guidelines?

2. What are Tommy's alternatives at this particular point in time?

3. Does the FTC have jurisdiction over advertising practices? Discuss.

4. How does the FTC action relate to Tommy's rights under the First Amendment to the Constitution?

5. Advise Tommy Tomison.

6. The FTC has specified standards for determining whether or not advertising messages are deceptive. Suggest some guidelines that you feel are reasonable.

7. Suggest what you think would be appropriate standards for endorsements, testimonials, and demonstrations.

CASE ANALYSIS

1. How should Tommy determine whether or not the advertisements in the series are in probable violation of the guidelines?

   Decision alternatives:

---

[1] This teaching note is from J. Barry Mason and Morris L. Mayer, Modern _Modern Retailing_ (Business Publications, 1981)

A. Tommy can have the advertisements evaluated by his counsel and staff and determine that the practices are probably not in violation of the standards or that they are probably violative.

B. Tommy can make the evaluation and preliminary determination himself based on his knowledge of the background and the law.

2. What are Tommy's alternatives at this particular point in time?

Decision alternatives:

A. Tommy could submit the materials requested voluntarily in the hope that cooperation would be the best route whether he thinks he has been in violation or not.

B. Tommy could withhold the materials requested until he is ordered to comply, whether he thinks he has been in violation or not.

C. Tommy can base his voluntary cooperation decision on the earlier determination; submit if probably not violative, withhold if violative.

3. Does the FTC have jurisdiction over advertising practices? Discuss.

Federal Trade Commission jurisdiction over advertising stems from section 5(a) of the Federal Trade Commission Act, 15 U.S.C. S45(a): prohibited practices include "unfair methods of competition in or affecting commerce, and unfair or deceptive acts or practices in or affecting commerce."

4. How does the FTC action relate to Tommy's rights under the First Amendment to the Constitution?

Although a new period in advertising regulation began with the series of Supreme Court decisions beginning in 1976, which held that commercial speech is protected by the First Amendment, certain forms of regulation remain permissible: restrictions as to time, place, and manner; and prohibitions of false and misleading statements. (See Virginia State Board of Pharmacy v. Va. Citizens Council, 425 United States 748; Bates v. State Bar of Arizona, 433 United States 350; Linmark Associates v. Willingboro, 431 United States 85; Carey v. Population Services International, 431 United States 678).

5. Advise Tommy Tomison.

Students have a great deal of leeway in the determination of this case. The first advertisement is probably deceptive in that it appears to be a demonstration of the actual practice; however, the use of the special attachment creates a misleading demonstration. This is clearly a prohibited practice.

The use of the female commentator is less clear-cut. In all honesty, it would be difficult to predict the judgement of the FTC staff on this aspect. Coupled with the other disallowed practice, this might also be

violative. However, because no actual endorsement occurs, it might well
be considered an acceptable use.

The second advertisement makes what might be considered as a health
claim; nontheless, because no specific standards are directly violated,
there is no probable cause for FTC action.

The third advertisement is clearly in actionable territory.
Children, given the FTC's position, are to be protected from such danger.
This ad then is the most directly non-protected.

Tommy's decision thus must be based on the assumption that he is in
violation of both fair trade practices and specific FTC guidelines.
Additionally, since there has been a history of FTC action, the company
will be guilty of repeat offenses. The only major potential limitation on
the power of the FTC to act is the effect the entire package of behavior
has had on the market.

Tommy must weigh this information against the perceived advantage of
voluntary response to the letter of complaint. His attorney would
probably advise waiting until the order was in hand before volunteering
any information. The student's decision must be based on the relative
advantage of time versus cooperation.

6. The FTC has specified standards for determining whether or not advertising
    messages are deceptive. Suggest some guidelines that you feel are
    reasonable.

    A. Need for intent or actual deception is unnecessary. (This has not
        been modified by the 1980 FTC Improvement Act.)

    B. Messages will be judged in their entirety for "total impression rule"
        governs.

    C. Literal truth will not serve as defense if deception is inherent.

    D. Advertisements are false if multiple meanings are possible and only
        one is false.

    E. Puffery is not actionable unless material objective statements are
        included.

    F. Advertisements directed at special audience groups will be interpreted
        on the basis of their probable meaning to members of that group. (The
        law protects "the public--the vast multitude which includes the
        ignorant, the unthinking and the credulous.") (See FTC v. Standard
        Education Society, 302 United States 113.)

7. Suggest what you think would be appropriate standards for endorsements,
    testimonials, and demonstrations.

    The FTC staff has been consistent in claiming that a reference to a
source of authority adds credibility such that high standards of
truthfulness and substantiation are applied.

A. If expertise is represented it must be real or explained.

B. Endorsements must always reflect the honest opinions, findings, beliefs, or experience of teh endorser.

C. Phrasing need not be exactly as given unless the advertisement so represents.

D. When use is represented, it must be a situation of bona fide use at the time the endorsement was given.

E. When actual use is indicated, the attributes of any product must be actual "run of line" products.

F. "Actual consumers" should be actual consumers; what the viewer thinks he sees should be actual.

G. Health, drug, or device claims must be provably valid.

H. Any material connections between endorser and manufacturer or distributor must be stated.

SANDWELL PAPER COMPANY[1]

CASE OBJECTIVES

1. This case illustrates the different problems that arise in industrial and wholesale selling situations. The salespeople in such a competitive environment requires extensive product and customer knowledge and carefully prepared sales techniques.

2. The case also emphasizes the importance of proper training and control procedures to keep a sales force functioning properly.

SUMMARY

Sandwell Paper Company wholesales both fine grade paper for printers and industrial grades for packing as well as complementary products which are carried by retailers (paper plates, napkins, etc.). Recently Sandwell has experienced a marked drop in profits although sales are climbing. Indeed, the number of new customers and orders has been increasing so rapidly that the sales force does not appear to be able to handle the volume of accounts and customers frequently have called the branch office to place orders and to request service. Still, margins are falling and Mr. Murphy, Bakersfield Branch Manager, does not think that the increasing price competitiveness of other area wholesalers is totally responsible. Therefore, he has requested an investigation of the effectiveness of the sales techniques utilized by his salespeople. Phil Edwards, a sales promotion staff member from the LA headquarters, has agreed to accompany the salespeople on their calls and observe their sales techniques.

QUESTIONS

1. Evaluate each of the sales presentations.

2. What training and control procedures would you implement?

3. Are there other changes which might improve salesperson performance at Sandwell?

CASE ANALYSIS

1. Evaluate each of the sales presentations.

    a. Bud Williams

---

[1]This teaching note is reproduced with the permission of its author Dr. Stuart V. Rich Professor of Marketing, and Director, Forest Industries Management Center, College of Business Administration, University of Oregon, Eugene, Oregon.

Bud's opening remark to Roy Mason ("What's up for today, Roy?") is very
weak. Bud should have opened with a presentation of a product Roy should
buy along with a prepared statement on the benefits Roy could gain from
it. Also, Bud does not exhibit sufficient confidence in the match-up of
Sandwell products and Roy's printing machinery. ("Well, so long as it's
going through the press okay" and "Medallion always runs good" in response
to a question about the paper's suitability to a specific press>) Bud
does not possess enough technical knowledge about Sandwell's product lines
and he knows it ("I try to keep up on the technical stuff but it is really
complicated," "I just can't defend it"). He also stalls any questions
about Sandwell's products and Roy's new press by promising to return with
a mill rep on another day. Such a weak stratagem reveals Bud's lack of
confidence in himself and forces him to make two calls on a client when
one should have been sufficient. Given Sandwell's recent increase in new
accounts, no Sandwell salesperson can waste time this way.

b.   Jane Austin

Again the initial contact with the customer is weak ("can we stock up your
bag, napkin, and container-cup inventories"). Jane should avoid the
suggestion that she is merely there to take down the usual order. Also,
she handled the customer's request for a price deal ineffectively. Her
failure to make a sale of Sandwell custodial products after 3 calls
suggests that she needs to prepare a stronger closing technique,
particularly one which overcomes a prospective customer's tendency to
delay finalizing the deal. She has definitely aided her sales
relationship with Jack Wilson by noticing that he had neglected to order
trays. She also makes the polyvinyl wrapping sale. But, like Bud, she
does not know enough about her product. She cannot tell Jack how long
chicken will keep in the new polyvinyl wrap: she merely assures him that
the wrap does not cause spoilage.

c.   Bob Thomas

Bob, too, subtly suggests that he is at Careways Market merely to collect
a re-order of products that Joe Martin already buys. Rather than
attempting to "sell" the display rack and demonstrating how effectively it
can be used, Bob simply asks if Joe wants more picnic items. He has
misdirected his sales effort: he knows Joe will buy the supplies, Bob
needs to sell the display case. Moreover, his reply that markup is 15% on
most items leaves Joe unclear as to how many carry that markup and which
products do not. When queried about how quickly items on the display rack
move, Bob lacks figures on dollar and unit volumes. Finally when Bob
demonstrated the new vinyl strapping Sandwell carries, he had not
practiced using the product and could not demonstrate it effectively. To
make matters worse, he then could not answer questions about the product's
strength and shipping characteristics.

2.   What training and control procedurs would you implement?

Sandwell salespeople appear to spend some time as telephone order takers
after their stint in the warehouse and before their field sales
experience. This fact is significant because George Murphy's salespeople
act more like telephone order takers than aggressive, well-prepared

salespeople. Their presentations lack creativity, depth of technical expertise, and finesse in sales techniques. Such qualities could be instilled by regular sales training meetings. During such meetings, techniques such as lecture, case analysis, coaching, role playing, demonstration, etc. would allow the salespeople to practice new product demonstrations and answers to difficult technical questions from customers. Experienced technical and promotion officers from LA headquarters can be scheduled into utilizing sessions to instruct the sales force about the technical aspects of the product, the technical aspects of machinery customers are using, and sales techniques. Sandwell would also be advised to include mill reps and salespeople from their important suppliers as part of their sales training program. These people are free instructors who will be happy to fill in Sandwell's salespeople on needed product knowledge. Such sales meetings must occur regularly (perhaps every 2 weeks) to allow the sales force to practice sales presentations, to be introduced to new promotional aids, and to be kept current on the production processes of their customers. The vital point, however, is that Sandwell salespeople need to become <u>selling</u> agents not remain walking order blanks.

3. <u>Are there other changes which might improve salesperson performance at Sandwell</u>?

Occasionally students feel that one of the salespeople profiled in the case should be fired. However, training and proper follow-up supervision should correct most problems with the sales force. Hiring another salesperson and redividing the customer load might be necessary if training does not help the sales force handle the increasing customer load. Another possible improvement Sandwell could institute is a compensation plan which varies commissions by product so that salespeople earn more for selling the more profitable items in the Sandwell line. Also Sandwell could increase the pricing authority of the sales force so that they can deal competitively in those markets where price is a significant selling tool. Finally, Sandwell can consider a redesign of this product lines, emphasizing the high margin items and eliminating the low margin products. Thus, the sales force can concentrate their efforts on those products which contribute most to bottom line profits.

COMPUTING SYSTEMS (CANADA)LIMITED[1]

CASE OBJECTIVES

1. To give students an opportunity to project themselves into the role of a young, ambitious field sales manager (who the students readily identify with) making a difficult decision about one of his salesmen in a relatively unstructured environment.

2. To demonstrate that an individual's competence in one particular job is not necessarily transferable to another job.

3. To illustrate some aspects of the salesman's activities in:
    a) Computer sales, in particular; and
    b) Technical products and services in general.

SUMMARY

In 1976, Bob Nichols, a young, highly competent systems representative with Computing Systems (Canada) Ltd., requested and was granted a transfer to sales. Except for his first year in sales, when he made an extremely large sale with the help of his superiors, Bob's performance as a sales representative has not been satisfactory. By February 1980, his district manager was wondering what should be done about Nichols. The district manager was new to his own job, very ambitious, and anxious to prove himself capable of handling all of the challenges of the position.

QUESTIONS

1. What task must a Computing Systems (Canada) Ltd. salesman perform and what qualities should a salesman possess in order to perform these tasks?

2. What are the tasks and attributes of a good systems analyst?

3. Based on the data in the case, what conclusions can be drawn about Bob Nichols? Is Bob suitable for the position of sales representative? Can his short-comings be corrected? How?

4. Under what constraints and pressures does Mike Hagen have to make his decision?

5. What options are open to Hagen? Evaluate each one.

6. What should Hagen do?

---

[1] This teaching note was prepared by Adrian B. Ryans. Copyright 1984 The University of Western Ontario.

CASE ANALYSIS

1. <u>Remembering that Mike Hagen was a highly successful salesperson, review
   his statement of the qualities which a successful CSL salesperson must
   possess.</u>

   a. Prospecting.

   To make CSL's sales quotas, each salesperson must be adept at developing
   large prospect lists. Sometimes they develop prospects by approaching the
   company on a cold call basis with a suggestion of a suitable computer
   system which the salespeople have designed to meet some need of the
   customer that they have perceived. However, the case states that CSL is
   more interested in customers who are aggressively seeking out computer
   services so that it appears that most of a CSL salesperson's prospecting
   duties consist of developing leads about companies in the market for
   computer services.

   b. Qualifying Prospects.

   Closely related to prospecting, qualifying means insuring that the
   customer is within 12 months of the actual purchase date. This involves
   getting access to the real decision makers in the client company, insuring
   that the customer will purchase CSL services within the 12 month time
   period, and choosing a contact in the company who can convince superiors
   of CSL quality if the CSL rep cannot gain access to the decision makers
   themselves. This step is vitally important because CSL is a smaller
   company in a hotly competitive business environment. CSL cannot afford to
   waste time on companies who are toying with the idea of computerization.

   c. Planning.

   Mike stresses that he finds it most difficult to get salespeople to plan.
   He emphasizes establishing projected closing dates and developing
   contingency plans to meet customer objections before the objections ever
   occur to the customer. By giving the entire campaign, from qualifying to
   closing, careful forethought, the salesperson can anticipate and pre-empt
   problems with a client.

   d. Closing.

   A successful CSL salesperson can sense when, and knows how, to "go for the
   jugular, that is, how to ask for the order aggressively." Mike calls it
   the "brass-knuckled approach."

   e. Assembling the Proper Support Team.

   Mike realizes that even the most conscientious salesperson cannot keep
   totally current in the technological advances in CSL products. Therefore,
   the successful salesperson knows both when to call for support personnel
   and which people to put on the team. But the successful assembling of a
   support team requires that the salesperson be able to "sell" the project
   to the technical people of CSL who will contribute to the team. Thus the

successful CSL salesperson is effective at both inside and outside selling tasks.

2. **In what ways does a good systems analyst differ from a successful salesperson?**

   a. Product Knowledge.

   Obviously, the analyst must possess a far greater understanding of the technological basis of both hardware and software than the salesperson requires. The analyst must be able to assemble that system which exactly matches the need of the client.

   b. Team Worker.

   First, the analyst must be able to work effectively with the CSL salesperson to design the best possible system for the client and maximize CSL's probability of making a sale. However, the analyst must allow be able to work closely with the client prior to the sale to determine the client's needs and design that system which best meets those needs. After the sale, the analyst must support the smooth implementation of the CSL system and see that the system lives up to the customer's expectations.

3. **Can Bob become a successful salesperson for CSL?**

   Mike Hagen fears that Bob is risk averse and therefore pulls his punches at the closing stage allowing clients either to slip through his fingers at the last moment or to negotiate ridiculously favorable closing terms for the client. Bob's lack of toughness is negotiating with clients is reflected in his inability to "sell" his proposals for deals to Computing Systems management. Finally, Mike worries that Bob lacks that killer instinct necessary for successful closing technique.

4. **What should Hagen do?**

   Both Hagen and CSL management regard Bob as too valuable an employee to ask for his resignation. However, it is unlikely that a transfer to another district will help Bob. Mike should establish some definite time period, for example six months, during which he will work closely with Bob and attempt to instill some of the qualities which Bob lacks. If, at the end of that time, Bob's sales performance shows no improvement then Bob should be directly confronted with a choice of a systems analyst position or a resignation.

ACTUAL DECISION

Mike persuaded Bob to accept a position as Large Systems Specialist for the Winnepeg District. For a while it appeared that Bob would get on well since he was obviously qualified for the position and Mike had arranged that Bob report directly to him rather than the systems manager with whom Bob might not get along. In his first year back in Systems Analysis, Bob won another company award. However, he left CSL a few months later to accept a sales job with a competitor.

WESTINGHOUSE ELECTRIC CORPORATION; OVERHEAD DISTRIBUTION TRANSFORMER DIVISION[1]

CASE OBJECTIVES

This case illustrates the several types of problems that can arise in the attempt to adequately train and motivate a sales force. Specifically, the objectives are: (1) to point out the need for sales training; (2) to call attention to some of the key problems in developing and maintaining a sales training program; (3) to show the relationship between sales training and salesperson productivity; (4) to permit a better understanding of the need for coordination of the different parts of a sales training program; (5) to investigate issues concerned with the proper timing of a change in a sales training program; (6) to analyze a specific approach to sales training.

SUMMARY

The Overhead Distribution Transformer Division (OHDT) of Westinghouse Electric Corporation had gone four years without any sort of formal training program for the field sales force. Sales force turnover had been 10 percent annually--much too high. It was evident that both the new and the veteran salespeople required more training. Feedback also indicated that the salespeople needed more depth in product knowledge and that this was crucial in light of intensely competitive conditions. The main problem facing Bob Ray, the marketing manager for OHDT, was to institute an effective sales training procedure that would help motivate the sales force to greater efforts.

QUESTIONS

Discussion can be opened by raising a variety of questions pertaining to sales training. For example:

1. What do you consider the "ideal" sales training program?

2. Is formal sales training necessary?

3. Should sales training be done before or after an individual is out on his or her own in the field?

4. What should a sales training program encompass (subject matter)?

5. What are the advantages and disadvantages of centralized and decentralized sales training?

---

[1]This teaching note was prepared by Norman A. P. Govoni, Babson College, Richard R. Still, California Polytechnic State University, and Kent Mitchell, University of Georgia.

6. Specifically, how can a large company find itself in a position such as Westinghouse when it comes to sales training?

CASE ANALYSIS

Basically, the Westinghouse problem revolves around the lack of a sound sales training mechanism which has resulted in the company's field sales force being somewhat short in product knowledge at a time of increased innovation and competition.

A. Westinghouse marketing personnel recognized a deficit in product knowledge possessed by their sales engineers, which could have long-run implications on future market share if left unchecked. Direct contact with and feedback from the sales force revealed this fact. Additionally, a predicted drop in market demand would likely cause the sales force to make more aggressive sales presentations to meet their own product loading in an environment where competition would be attempting to retain or increase its own market share. With a possible decrease in demand, purchasing agents would have cause to scrutinize the products even more closely. Since there are competitors who produce a similar product, the sales engineers must be equipped to relate the value story behind the Westinghouse product.

B. To resolve the problem, the marketing department has created a training campaign called "The Problem Solvers" which is targeted to the sales engineers and their managing chain. The campaign catches attention with the mailing of expensive adult puzzle games based on the theme, "The Problem Solvers," and it includes cover letters, information brochures, and a simple crossword puzzle to be partially completed with each of the five mailings. The final mailing contains a cover letter, a sales presentation summary, and a flip chart sales aid.

C. As time progresses, several decisions relative to training have to be made. Two of the many decisions that will have to be made by the marketing manager and hi staff are:

1. The timing of mailing intervals and the feedback mechanism.

    Using two-month intervals, even if only four or five mailings were to be used, seems questionable. There is a risk that over such a long period initial objectives and appeal of the campaign could become hazy or, indeed, forgotten. The long mailing intervals could be misinterpreted by the target to mean that OHDT does not invite immediate use of, or concentrated attention to the program's real goals. Also, the major utilities, representing the largest purse, would be the testing ground for campaign effectiveness. If the mailings were shortened to, say, three-week intervals, the testing ground would become the smaller, low-volume consumer, and the sales force would have had the chance to test their newly found knowledge on less critical customers. This could provide two results: first, the salespeople would be less hesitant and more confident about using their new training with the big utilities toward the end of the year; and, second, the OHDT marketing department would be able to compare the short-run feedback (the completed crossword puzzles) with the long-range feedback (increased sales/less product questions) and make adjustments in the form of a newsletter, if considered necessary.

2. Disposition of future newcomers to the sales force.

A 10 percent turnover of sales personnel was one of the causes of the present training campaign. Odds are, that a few years from now, a new training program or public relations program will be reseeded by OHDT. Numerous factors will probably cause this (such as, innovations, sales decline, market trends, and so forth).

However, in isolating the new salesperson, it is known that he or she tends to have better sales in the area he or she knows best. To make sure the salesperson has a lasting "impression" of OHDT, a special effort should be made to keep the sales force fully informed during the interim of campaigns. OHDT could create a compacted model of the "Problem Solvers" and forward it under the pretext that the salesperson would benefit from better product knowledge. An example of this would be the following: one adult game, an impressive cover letter, all of the present Problem Solver bulletins, and sales presentation aids. The feedback mechanism (the crossword puzzles) could be kept the same or changed depending on the feedback results of the original campaign. The package could come to the new salesperson unannounced or by preannounced "hit" from his or her area sales manager in Athens.

These issues provide an indication of the types of questions that can be pursued. Essentially, the issues boil down to the critical need for sales training and how to develop and maintain a sales training program that does its job and which has full support of the sales force.

ADDITIONAL REFERENCES

There are several good books on selling and sales management that will provide insight into the types of problems faced by Westinghouse. Among the books are:

Enis, Ben M., _Personal Selling_. Santa Monica: Goodyear, 1979 (Chapters 11-14)

Shapiro, Benson P., _Sales Program Management_. New York: McGraw-Hill, 1976 (Sections 2, 8, 11).

Stanton, William J., and Richard H. Buskirk, _Management of the Sales Force_. Homewood, Ill.: Richard D. Irwin, 1978 (Chapters 8, 9, 15).

FOOD DYNAMICS[1]

CASE OBJECTIVES

The purpose of this case is to provide a springboard that facilitates the discussion of sales compensation and the role they play in motivating sales personnel.

SUMMARY

This case deals with compensation programs. Food Dynamics Inc. was created when three salespeople left a large New England food brokerage firm in hopes of starting their own business. One major concern of the firm was loosing good sales people. This motivated the three owners to develop a compensation plan that would inspire loyalty. This was accomplished by giving the people they hired a stake in the company by tying commissions to the salesperson's contribution to overall profits. Under their system, a salesperson would not only develop his sales territory, but also take charge of maximizing the territory's profitability for the firm, in return for a percentage of the profits.

The results of Food Dynamic's approach to managing their people has been a large success financially. Annual sales are currently $30 million, and the top 22 food manufactures are represented.

QUESTIONS

1. Evaluate the compensation program at Food Dynamics.

2. Is sales management doing a good job of motivating the sales force?

ANALYSIS

1 . Evaluate the compensation program at Food Dynamics.

While no compensation plan meets all the criteria for the ideal plan, Food Dynamics has a good approach for their objectives. Although the case does not so state, it appears that the principals have been very thorough in the recruiting and selection of sales personnel. To keep personnel loyal, etc., the first step must be good selection.

The ideal compensation program would have certain characteristics.

(1) It would be simple.

---

[1] These teaching notes are based on materials provided by William G. Zikmund and Michael d'Amico ,**MARKETING** (New York, John Wiley and sons, 1986).

Food Dynamics' program is not simple, but with veteran and quality salespeople, this would not present a major problem.

(2) It would be fair.

The program appears to be fair. The expense allocation and percentage of profit payments are "agreed upon" figures. When unusual expenses occur within a territory, adjustments are made.

(3) It would provide regular income.

The salary plus the bonus provides a regular flow of income.

(4) It would provide security to the salesperson, but give incentive to work.

The payment program yields both of these, particularly in the short-term. The long-term may present problems. If a territory is profitable and the salesperson is satisfied with his/her income, the incentive to increase sales and profitability is reduced.

(5) It would provide sales management with some control over the salesperson's activities and develop long-term profitable relationships with clients.

This plan does quite well. The goal and payment schedule is based on such relationships. A variety of activities assist assist in establishing these relationships.

(6) It would encourage optimal purchase orders by the customer.

Again, the plan is profit based, so optimal orders are ideal.

2. Is sales management doing a good job of motivating the sales force?

Food Dynamics appears to have a good compensation program, however, financial incentives are not the only motivators of a salesperson. Many salespeople are high achievement-oriented individuals and may seldom require supervision from sales managers. For these people, selling itself is highly motivating. Despite these excitements and the feeling of being of service to clients, most salespeople need at least occasional support from management. Food Dynamics' management recognizes this. They know that sales personnel are often subject to broad fluctuations in morale and motivation. The partners provide support by working with their salespeople, in the field and at trade shows. Training is provided to develop the skills and knowledge of each employee. Management-employee contact is made on a regular basis. It is possible, however, to have too much contact. Three or four phone contacts a day are a bit much. Gavin says "they (the salespeople) don't feel we are checking up on them." The statement may be true, but it is doubtful that salespeople feel this way.

That many phone calls would get old fast. The results have been good for the last six years. The proof, however, will be the next six years.

NATIONAL ENERGY DEVICES, INC[1]

CASE OBJECTIVES

1. To illustrate the types of distribution problems a company, especially a new company, has in getting its product accepted into the distribution network.

2. To show the importance of distribution in marketing strategy and how all elements of the system have to be in place for marketing success.

SUMMARY

This case involves a distribution system that is not working as effectively as expected in that sales to one market segment are well below expectations. National Energy Devices, Inc., markets its products to both commercial and residential customers. The main emphasis, however, was their residential customers. NED's main product was an energy devise called the "FuelSaver". This device served as a vehicle for introducing platinum into a furnace's combustion process, resulting in the release of more heat with a reduction of fuel consumption.

The energy saving business appeared to be an extremely large and lucrative industry. This attracted many new competitors to infiltrate the industry, causing stiff competition. As a result, sales have been lower than expected.

QUESTIONS

1. Evaluate the distribution strategy currently employed by National Energy Devices.

2. What factors should be considered by Mr. Howard in further developing NED's distribution network?

3. What suggestions can you make in order to assist NED in overcoming the recent adverse publicity relative to energy saving devices?

4. How can NED best attempt to grow and prosper given its present condition?

CASE ANALYSIS

1. Evaluate the distribution strategy currently employed by National Energy Devices.

The FuelSaver is a durable good, somewhat complex, and early in its life cycle. In this situation a direct distribution channel is called for and NED chose the applicable method by directing some of its effort on a door-to-door basis. In addition, it is approaching middlemen on a selective basis which will maintain channel goodwill once the product is established. Its choice on type of middlemen is accurate in that the FuelSaver is logically allied with the products and services tied to its

---

[1]. From Norman Gouoni S.P. Jeanette and H.N. Deneault, Cases in Marketing Copyright c 1983. John Wiley & Sons. Reprinted with permission.

128

function, oil burner sales and service companies. They can provide the technical know-how to support the product in the field.

2. **What factors should be considered by Mr. Howard in further developing NED's distribution network?**

   In the selection of middlemen he should be concerned with:

   - Do they have conflicting lines or products which will limit our potential in the operation?
   - Do they have complementary products which can aid our products sales?
   - Are they willing and able to push the product?
   - Do they have adequate sales and service personnel?
   - Do they have the courage to maintain reasonable margins when times are tough?
   - Are they adequately financed and making profits?
   - Will a commitment to a particular middleman limit potential in a particular marketing area?

   He should also be considering other forms of outlets such as Home Improvement Centers.

3. **What suggestions can you make in order to assist NED in overcoming the recent adverse publicity relative to energy saving devices?**

   Although the industry is in an infant stage, it is possible that there is a grade association which can generate some favorable publicity and act as a spokesperson for the legitimate members of the industry. NED should attempt to contact this association for assistance.

   The firm has testimonials to the benefits of the FuelSaver which should be publicized through local media as well as used for sales presentation material. NED should also consider participation in consumer oriented shows or exhibits in order to increase exposure for the product.

4. **How can NED best attempt to grow and prosper given its present condition?**

   What NED needs to succeed in the consumer market is a seal of approval from the Brookhaven test facility and some time for the adverse publicity to dissipate. In order to convince middlemen to push the product NED must demonstrate proven performance. In order to do either of the above Mr. Howard must generate some cash and keep the product moving. The option of selling his stock to finance an advertising campaign is plausible but probably not necessary.

   Given that the test results from Bookhaven are at least 8 months away and he has had little success attracting middlemen to push his product, a penetration price policy with the segment where he has had the most success is the best possible approach. The variable cost of this unit is about $60.00, (including the platinum catalyst), and he has been selling them to realtors at $200.00, a respectable margin in any business, yet well below the suggested retail of $495.00. To discount the product at the consumer or middleman level now will only generate suspicion and hurt his image with the middlemen at a later date. He should concentrate his total sales effort in the area where his price will be least publicized, where he can sell units in quantity to generate cash, and where he can show an established record of performance to potential middlemen at a later date.

ADDITIONAL QUESTIONS FOR DISCUSSION

1. What other products can be used to forecast the development path of fuel saving devices such as the FuelSaver?

2. What future do you see for the fuel saving industry?

THOMPSON RESPIRATION PRODUCTS, INC.[1]

SUMMARY

Thompson Respiration Products, Inc. (TRP) is a small (1981 revenues of $3.0 million) manufacturer of portable respirators. Portable respirators are used by people whose natural breathing function has been severely impaired or lost. TRP began its operation (and the industry) around 1950 and was virtually the only competitor until the 1970s. However, by April 1982, TRP's market share based on new units shipped had declined to approximately 10%. The firm now faced two primary and several secondary competitors.

Higgins, the Executive Vice President, must resolve six rather immediate distribution issues, as stated in the case's last section:

1. Should TRP continue to rent respirators to dealers?

2. Should TRP protect each dealer's territory (and how big should a territory be)?

3. Should TRP require dealers to stock no competing equipment?

4. How many dealers should TRP eventually have? Where?

5. What sales information should be assembled in order to attract high quality dealers?

6. What should be done about the "best efforts" clause?

In essence, Higgins must rapidly (the need for urgency is justified in this note) find capable dealers, convince them to carry TRP products, and motivate them to push TRP products. The case's second paragraph raises another immediate issue, Higgins' lack of time. The case's last paragraph raises strategic considerations that students should address before they attack immediate issues.

Discussion on all these points is not possible in one class period. Thus, the instructor should be prepared to focus the class's attention on selected issues and to recognize that remaining issues be merely identified. Resolution of this latter set of issues makes an excellent follow-up assignment, to be completed as a short paper. An alternative, of course, is to teach the case over two class periods.

Learning Objectives

TRP was written to teach students:

1. Channels of distribution decisions require quantitative and qualitative analyses of buyers, competitors, and the company itself.

---

[1].These teaching notes were prepared by Professor James E. Nelson, University of Colorado.

2. Some marketing problems require that managers take quick, dramatic action.

3. Innovative organizations generally stand to receive the lion's share of rewards available in a market.

4. Market power in a channel of distribution may rest with the manufacturer or retailer (or wholesaler) as the channel captain.

5. Large, powerful manufacturers may avoid small markets that show similarities with currently served, large markets--until the small markets grow or the large markets decline.

These and other insights that follow from class discussion might be presented by the instructor at the end of the period.

Teaching Suggestions

Class discussion will work best when students begin by analyzing TRP, consumers, and competitors. After subtleties hidden in these topic areas surface, discussion can profitably focus on resolving selected case issues. The instructor would usually begin discussion either with TRP or consumers, with a request similar to, "Tell me about TRP (or TRP's consumers)>"

Alternatively, the case has been used as an examination in a three-hour class period with instructions as follows:

Read the Thompson Respiration Products, Inc. case. Answer these three questions.

1. Summarize your view of the situation facing Thompson Respiration Products, Inc. Your summary may include simple restatements of case facts in addition to detailed qualitative and quantitative analyses. Your summary should be complete in terms of marketing concepts.

2. State your recommendations on either issue 2 or 3 or 6 (appearing in the last section of the case). Be succinct. Be clear.

Support your recommendations with references to your summary in 1 above.

3. State one other marketing related recommendation that you would give to Higgins which deals with issues other than those identified in the case's last section.

Support this recommendation in 4 or 5 sentences.

Obviously, instructors could substitute other case issues from the case's last section for those identified in question 2a.

Summarize the Situation: TRP

Students might estimate that TRP grosses the following annual per unit revenues (from case Exhibit 6).

	Transaction	
Customer Class	Rent	Sell
dealers	$2,400	$3,000
patients	$3,000	$4,000

However, TRP earns the estimated rental revenues only when it rents the unit for an entire 12 month period. On the average, then, a new unit rented to dealers or to patients in 1981 will produce revenues half those listed above. Thus, TRP's revenues of $3.0 million and shipments of 465 units in 1981 may be broken down as follows (assigning exactly half of total revenues to dealers, half to patients, as the case states).

1981 Sales Performance

Customer class	$(000)	units
dealers	540	180
patients	60	15

1981 Rental Performance

		units	
	$(000)	new	old
dealers	960	120	(340)
patients	1,440	150	(405)
Total	$3,000	465	745

Units in parentheses are easily estimated by subtracting from total rental revenue these rental revenues derived from new rental units:

($1,200).120 or $144,000 (for dealers)
($1,500).150 or $225,000 (for patients)

and dividing the two amounts remaining by $2,400 (for dealers) and $3,000 (for patients).

At first glance, data appear to conflict with a statement in the case that units last about three to five years in the field. That is, TRP's unit breakdown for 1981 as above indicates total revenues derived from 465 new units and 745 old units, implying that the average life is 745/465 or 1.6 years. However, some of the 465 units are undoubtedly purchased by new dealers as inventory. Further, Higgins knows that the industry is growing at 3% per year. If he estimates that 65 units are due to pipeline filling and to natural growth, he could then estimate that of 1145 TRP units (400 + 745) operating in the field, 400 or about one-third are less than one year old (averaging, in fact, one-half year of age).

Two conclusions follow from this sales analysis. (1) TRP can dangle a $1.5 million carrot in front of prospective dealers, in the form of revenues TRP currently derives each year directly from patients. (2) Sale of patients' rental units and the accompanying stream of payments to dealers will involve a negotiated price between TRP and dealers. The end result will likely be a one-time payment to TRP of some two to three times its current annual patient rental revenues and a reduction in TRP's annual revenue to $1.5 million.

Further class discussion directed at TRP should disclose that the firm quite likely offers too many respirator models. This idea of excessive product proliferation is supported by considering the limited number of models offered by competitors, experience curves, and TRP's gross margin of 35%. If TRP can cut its costs of production, say, 10% via increased experience, gross margin rises to 40%, a 17% increase.

Students might also analyze the possibility that TRP hire someone whose primary responsibility would be to seek new dealers. A rough estimate of expenses would be:

salary	$25,000	
fringe benefits	10,000	
travel expenses	25,000	(20 weeks at $1,250/week)
	$60,000	

Using, say, $1,000 as an estimate of TRP's current per unit gross margin, Higgins would calculate the break even point at 60 units. This represents a 12.9% increase in sales (60/465).

Students should estimate that TRP's current market share is around 10%. The case states that life expectancies of both respirators and patients are about five years and that each patient would usually rent or own two respirators. About 4200 of these respirators will fail or become obsolete during the year. About 2100 of these patients will die, freeing up about 4200 respirators. Thus, the existing market can essentially be seen as a wash, demanding as many respirators as it supplies. The 2200 new patients each year require about 4400 respirators. Thus, TRP's current market share is about 465/4400 or 10.6%. Student estimates will vary, depending on their assumptions and rigor.

Finally, TRP has a relatively new distribution network consisting of 3 large dealers and 18 small dealers (disregarding Metro who just signed). TRP performance at each dealer category may be calculated as:

Dealer Category	New Sales (units)	(ave.)	New Rental (units)	(ave.)	Old Rental (units)	(ave.)
large (N=3)	110	37	70	23	200	67
small (N=18)	70	4	50	3	140	10

To simplify summary calculations, assume that dealers only rent units to patients (at $3,000 per year for old units and at $1,500 for the first year of a new unit). Thus, the average large dealer grosses ($3,000)(67) + ($1,500)(37+23) or $291,000 each year on Thompson respirators. The average small dealer grosses only ($3,000)(10) + ($1,500)(4+3) or $40,500. Both estimates assume old units are rented 12 months out of the year.

Summarize the Situation: Buyers

Patients using portable respirators would typically come from all income, occupation, education, and subcultural groups. They would tend to concentrate disproportionately in metropolitan areas because of the availability of specialized medical care. According to statements in the case, the entire U>S> market of 10,500 home respirator patients could be broken into 8,300 old and 2,200 new patients, requiring 16,600 and 4,400 respirators respectively. On the average, dealers would have grossed in 1981 $3,000 and $1,500 per each old and new respirator unit, respectively (assuming that all patients rented), making a retail market of $56.4 million. Charges for service calls and rental of related equipment would increase this figure.

Almost all patients would choose their respirator solely on the advice of some medical expect--either a physician or a respiration therapist. In effect, patients would exercise no decision criteria and would defer to the technical expert. The decision maker probably would consider patient suitability or fit, reliability, after-sales service, and delivery as key decision criteria. Price would not be a factor as long as it was in a reasonable range. In fact, the decision maker may hold a strong price-quality relationship and refuse to consider respirators that are priced too low.

The decision maker is likely quite aware of the superior features possessed by hospital style respirators. He or she will keep current via trade and professional journals, contact with dealers and manufacturers, and contact with associates. Most decision makers will work in large general hospitals, spinal cord injury centers, pulmonary disease treatment centers, medical schools, or respiration therapy schools. Most decision makers will require detailed personal conversations in order to convince them to recommend a respirator of a manufacturer other than their current preference.

Students should also consider prospective dealers as buyers. As the case describes, prospective dealers will currently employ one or more respiration therapists who service patients with emphysema, bronchitis, asthma, and other respiratory ailments. (Students should estimate the size of this market as some 10 times greater than that for portable respirators.) Competition between dealers is likely strong, given Higgins' statement in the case's second paragraph that over 100 dealers currently operate in Minneapolis and Atlanta.

Dealers in each market area may show an interest in carrying portable respirators but only until one or two other dealers pick up the line. Once this occurs, all remaining prospective dealers will consider their opportunity to earn profits greatly diminished. T see this, students might consider a city of 2 million residents and estimate the potential market at:

$$\frac{2 \text{ million}}{230 \text{ million U.S.}} \cdot 10,500 \text{ patients} = 90 \text{ patients on respirators}$$

$$\frac{2 \text{ million}}{230 \text{ million U.S.}} \cdot \$56.4 \text{ million} = \$480,000 \text{ market revenues}$$

$$\frac{2 \text{ million}}{230 \text{ million U.S.}} \cdot 16,600 \text{ old respirators} = 140 \text{ old respirators}$$

$$\frac{2 \text{ million}}{230 \text{ million U.S.}} \cdot 4,400 \text{ new respirators} = 40 \text{ new respirators}$$

If two dealers currently rent portable respirators in the market but do so poorly that one-third of the market is easily gained by a new competitor, the new competitor would earn revenues of $480,000/3 or about $160,000. However, if instead the two existing dealers compete such that only one-tenth of the old market and only one-fourth of the new market is captured, the new competitor will gross only:

$$(.10) \ (140) \ (\$3,000) + (.25) \ (40) \ (\$1,500) = \$57,000$$

Given that most dealers' annual revenues are between $5 and $10 million, a $57,000 revenue increase would be seen as insignificant.

Students should also conclude that most dealers will be reluctant to carry two competing lines of portable respirators. Portable respirators will represent a sideline and (for the sake of simplicity and from the lack of strong concern) most dealers will not seek two sources of supply. However, prospective dealers might compare TRP to Life Products and note the latter firm's higher suggested rental rates and limited product line. Both distinctions may be important advantages: the higher suggested rental rates will likely not put off many MDs and RTs and will allow the dealer to earn higher per unit dollar margins; the more limited product line means the dealer would stock less inventory and simplify service.

Somewhere in this discussion the concept of channel power should arise. Students should conclude that power lies primarily with the dealer. Dealers are larger than TRP, posses unique knowledge about their local markets, view portable respirators as a sideline, and may buy from two competing suppliers (TRP and Life Products). Large regional and national chains possess the most channel power.

Finally, students should be pressed to comment on the urgency of TRP's securing a strong dealer network. TRP will find it difficult to enter any market where Life Products and Lifecare Services already compete, if existing dealers compete aggressively. To see this, students might estimate that the entire U.S. market can support upwards of 225 dealers, by assuming a dealer on the average would want to earn at least $250,000 in annual revenues from portable respirators ($56.4 million/$250,000 = 225). As the case states, TRP, Life Products, and Lifecare Services already have 22, "over 40," and 17 (16 field offices plus its headquarters) dealers, respectively. Whichever firm gets the best of the 150 or so remaining dealers first will have the best chance of success. A strategic window is open--but sliding shut.

Summarize the Situation: Competitors

TRP directly competes with Life Products and Lifecare Services. Life Products has over 40 dealers in large metropolitan areas, all of which have signed distribution agreements since 1976. Life Products currently offers two respirator models and a limited number of accessories, at suggested rental rates some 1.6 to 2.0 times greater than those listed by TRP. Having fewer models implies that Life Products may produce units more efficiently than TRP because of experience curve effects. In sum, Life Products seems an aggressive, technologically capable, and well managed firm.

Lifecare Services has 16 wholly owned field offices plus its headquarters as its dealer network. Despite the expense of this system, Lifecare Services did not sell but instead rented (its single respirator model plus some old TRP models), at rates approximately 70% of those for TRP. Lifecare Services' limited product line, licensing agreement, and smaller dealer network imply that it is a lesser competitor.

Students might also note the possibility of one or more of the four manufacturers of hospital-style respirators deciding to enter the portable respirator market. These "latent competitors" likely possess the technology, personnel, and capital to pose a serious threat should they decide to compete. However, students might question the ability of their dealer networks to sell directly to patients and to provide the accompanying service.

Strategic Issue: TRP's Marketing Objectives

As the case's last paragraph states, Higgins plans to reflect on: "the nature of the target market, a statement of marketing objectives, and TRP's possible entry into the hospital market." This note already has extensively discussed the target market as the earlier "Buyers" section. From this and all other note discussions to here, TRP marketing objectives might be stated as:

1. Provide the portable respirator market with a technologically superior product.

2. Develop a network of 100 strong dealers in large metropolitan areas in the U.S. (and Canada).

3. Support dealers with frequent personal contacts, high margins, and high quality products.

4. Inform MDs/RTs of TRP's product advantages and local availability.

TRP should take several immediate and dramatic actions consistent with these objectives--to delay invites disaster.

Strategic Issue: Enter the Hospital Market?

Students will make several points as reasons to enter the hospital market:

1. TRP's dealers likely already call on hospital MDs and RTs.

2. TRP's rental terms may be seen by hospital purchasing agents as an important feature (but are purchasing agents also decision makers?).

3. Compared to Life Products' portable respirators, TRP's more accurate pressure monitoring and easier volume adjustments might be a significant advantage in hospital applications.

4. MDs/RTs exposed to TRP respirators in hospitals are more likely to recommend the products for home use.

Students might identify these as reasons to avoid the hospital market:

1. Before it can enter the hospital market, TRP needs a strong dealer network. Many hospitals will insist on local service representation.

2. TRP currently lacks sufficient personnel to establish the dealer network, much less to support dealer sales or direct sales to hospitals.

3. To enter the hospital market might induce manufacturers of hospital-style respirators to enter the portable market.

4. Life Products already seems to be entering the hospital market, based on a statement made by one of their executives.

On balance, TRP probably should enter the hospital market but only after its dealer network becomes better established.

Answers to the Six Distribution Issues

Should TRP continue to rent respirators to dealers?

Reasons for:

1. Rental is more profitable than selling. Rental revenues for the M3000, for example, will exceed the unit's selling price after only 16 months ($4,500/$290 = 15.5 months).

2. Rental allows dealers to avoid an initial cash investment and to dismiss any fears of technological product obsolescence.

3. Rental allows dealers to hold a large inventory of TRP products.

4. TRP's rental terms differentiate it from Life Products on one more dimension.

Reasons against:

1. Rental slows cash flow to TRP and increases the need for expensive working capital (an opportunity here for the instructor to comment on the link between marketing decisions and financial decisions).

2. Rental is contrary to industry practice.

3. Rental may slow TRP's technological innovation (because it slows cash flow and makes TRP fear technological obsolescence).

4. Rental complications TRP bookkeeping and internal control activities.

5. Rental may result in conflict between TRP and its dealers. Dealers, for example, may pay late, sell an occasional rental unit without telling TRP, and abuse rental units.

6. Dealers might push TRP products harder if inventory were owned.

On balance, TRP probably should discontinue its policy of renting respirators to dealers.

Should TRP protect each dealer's territory (and how big should a territory be)?

Starting with the second question, a dealer's territory should be large enough to allow it to earn substantial revenue. Otherwise, TRP will account for such a small part of revenue that the dealer will lose interest. The exact revenue figure is debatable. Suppose students agree that a dealer should earn "around a quarter of a million dollars." Assuming that all patients rent (two units, at $3,000 each), a territory must have $250,000/$6,000 or about 40 patients to interest a dealer. Thus, students might derive the following schedule:

Territory Population	Expected Number of Patients*	Maximum Number of Dealers
1 million	45	1.1
2 million	90	2.2
3 million	135	3.4
4 million	180	4.5
5 million	225	5.6
6 million	270	6.8
7 million	315	7.9
8 million	360	9.0
9 million	405	10.1
10 million	450	11.2

* $\frac{1 \text{ million}}{230 \text{ million U.S.}}$ 10,500 patients = 45 patients

Concerning the first question, TRP probably should attempt to protect a dealer's territory, as long as the dealer performs well. These reasons may be given as support:

1. Dealers possess most of the power in the channel and may demand territorial protection as a condition to carry the TRP line.

2. TRP would prefer that a territory contain one large TRP dealer rather than two or three small ones (assuming TRP derives equal sales revenues in the territory). Larger dealers will be more aggressive, more likely to provide service, and more aware of TRP's contribution to their own revenues and profits.

3. TRP may use the promise to protect a dealer's territory as a quid pro quo for the dealer's promise to adhere to the best efforts clause.

4. Consumer demand is consistent with exclusive distribution.

On the other hand, TRP should take care that territorial protection does not lead to dealer complacency.

Students might recognize that Higgins probably can legally restrict the territories of TRP dealers (see John F. Cady, "Reasonable Rules and Rules of Reason: Vertical Restrictions on Distributors," and Saul Sands and Robert J. Posch, Jr., "A Checklist of Questions for Firms Considering a Vertical Territorial Distribution Plan," both in the Summer 1982 issue of the Journal of Marketing. Students should also note that Higgins cannot promise existing TRP dealers that a nearby chain dealer would not gain the TRP line via a decision made at the chain's corporate headquarters. About all Higgins can do is assure existing TRP dealers that he will not actively seek another dealer in a territory as long as the existing dealer aggressively supports the TRP line.

Should TRP require dealers to stock no competing equipment?

Reasons for keeping the requirement:

1. TRP will get greater dealer push; TRP will have more influence with each dealer.

2. TRP's lower suggested rental rates imply longer dealer paybacks. Consequently, if Higgins allowed dealers to carry the Life Products line also, dealers would push the more profitable line.

3. The requirement has to date not seemed burdensome--TRP has signed 22 dealers over the past "year or so," a faster rate than the one for Life Products (over 40 dealers signed in six years).

4. If TRP protects the dealer's territory, it is reasonable to ask that the dealer agree to sell only the TRP line.

Reasons against:

1. Some dealers oppose the requirement; large chains especially may see it as a barrier to signing a TRP Dealer Agreement.

2. Most dealers won't sell but one line of portable respirators anyway; consequently the requirement is not really ;needed.

3. A direct in-store comparison between the TRP and Life Products lines by an MD/RT will benefit TRP because of TRP's broader product line and its unique product features (and lower rental rates?).

4. TRP probably cannot enforce the requirement anyway because of its lack of channel power.

On balance, TRP probably should keep the requirement--but willingly strike it from a contract when a strong prospective dealer expresses this desire.

How many dealers should TRP eventually have? Where?

Marketing objective 1 earlier in this note stated a desire for 100 dealers, approximately 45% of the 225 feasible for the nation. Students might identify, say, the top 100 markets in the country on the basis of population, estimate the number of patients in each market, and use the preceding schedule as a guide to the number of dealers. Table 1 at the end of these notes gives data for the 30 largest SMSAs, suitable for reproduction (TRP might aim for 40 dealers in these markets). The instructor might note the appropriateness of students' seeking secondary data in solving marketing problems.

Beyond the SMSAs in Table 1, students should urge that TRP find dealers located near schools that train MDs and RTs, near spinal cord injury centers, and near pulmonary disease treatment centers.

What sales information should be assembled in order to attract high quality dealers?

Students might develop a list of sales information (beyond the existing technical specification sheets and price list) under headings of "Local Market Related Information" and "TRP Related Information."

Local Market Related Information	TRP Related Information
estimated number of patients	company background, history
estimated respirator market potential $	durability, safety record
estimated related products market potential $	service intervals, procedures
competing dealers	breadth of product line
locations	terms of sale
strengths, weaknesses	sample TRP Dealer Agreement
estimated dealer costs necessary to	trade histories of TRP
service the market	dealers

Students will develop similar lists. Care should be taken that the lists contain information in a form that will appeal to dealers, i.e., lists should be dealer oriented, not product oriented.

What should be done about the "best efforts" clause?

Reasons to keep the clause:

1. The clause is consistent with TRP's desired image as a high quality supplier.

2. The clause plainly identifies activities that TRP expects at a minimum from its dealers (and the clause allows TRP an explicit basis with which to terminate a dealer).

3. The clause is not unreasonable (see the last paragraph in this section).

Reasons to drop the clause:

1. TRP lacks sufficient resources to enforce the clause.

2. Some prospective dealers may see the clause as sufficiently burdensome to lose interest in TRP.

Instead of merely arguing to keep or to drop the clause, more perceptive students will suggest that Higgins take other actions. They might organize their comments by referring to specific parts of the best efforts clause. As examples:

1. Higgins might point out to dealers that their initial <u>investment in TRP inventory</u> should be less than $10,000 and be recovered in less

than 16 months (based on calculations from case Exhibit 6; the dealers, however, expect a payback in 12 months or less--should TRP's price structure be changed?). Higgins might also point out that a sale lost for lack of inventory is lost forever, based on the nature of the patient's purchase situation.

2. <u>Four contacts per month</u> (suppose at two hours each) would probably cost the dealer less than $200 per month. TRP could partially reimburse dealers--as an incentive program in force for part of each year.

3. TRP could support dealers by sending <u>a factory representative to major conventions</u> and by partially reimbursing dealers for exhibition expenses.

Marketing Plan

As noted in the case's last paragraph, Higgins hopes to have a strategic marketing plan in place before July. Students might be asked to draft such a plan as a major written assignment. They might use a format suggested by Williams and Neuhaus, "A Model for a Strategic Marketing Plan," page 523 in the 1977 AMA Proceedings.

What Happened

As of February 1983, Higgins had trimmed four models from the TRP line. He had signed an additional six independent dealers and two more regional chains, to make a total of 51 TRP dealers in the U.S. and Canada. He was actively seeking a TRP sales or dealer manager whose primary responsibility would be to secure and maintain a 100-dealer network. Concerning the immediate case issues, TRP:

1. continued to rent respirators to dealers.

2. continued to protect dealer territories.

3. dropped its requirement that dealers stock no competing equipment.

4. hoped to have 70 dealers under contract by the end of 1983 (by hiring a manager charged with this responsibility and by focusing her or his efforts on large chains).

5. deferred assembling any sales information, pending the hiring of this individual.

6. deferred any decision on the best efforts clause, pending the hiring of this individual.

Finally, Higgins decided not to enter the hospital market for the reasons cited earlier.

Table 1, Largest 30 SMSAs

SMSA	Estimated 1982 Population (000,000)	Estimated Number of: Patients	Dealers
New York	9.0	405	10.1
Los Angeles/Long Beach	7.6	345	8.6
Chicago	7.2	325	8.1
Philadelphia	4.7	210	5.5
Detroit	4.3	195	4.9
San Francisco/Oakland	3.3	150	3.8
Houston	3.2	150	3.8
Washington, D.C.	3.1	140	3.5
Dallas/Ft. Worth	3.1	140	3.5
Boston	2.7	120	3.0
Nassau-Suffolk, N.Y.	2.6	120	3.0
St. Louis	2.3	105	2.6
Baltimore	2.3	105	2.6
Pittsburgh	2.3	105	2.6
Minneapolis/St. Paul	2.2	100	2.5
Atlanta	2.1	95	2.4
Anaheim/Santa Ana	2.1	95	2.4
San Diego	2.0	90	2.2
Newark	1.9	85	2.1
Cleveland	1.9	85	2.1
Miami	1.7	75	1.9
Seattle	1.7	75	1.9
Riverside, CA	1.7	75	1.9
Denver/Boulder	1.7	75	1.9
Tampa/St. Petersburg	1.7	75	1.9
Phoenix	1.6	70	1.8
Milwaukee	1.5	65	1.6
Cincinnati	1.4	60	1.5
San Jose	1.3	60	1.5
Kansas City	1.3	60	1.5
TOTALS	85.5	3855	96.7

GOODBUY SUPERMARKET[1]

CASE OBJECTIVES

1. To understand the factors involved in the decision to expand through new outlets.

2. To give the student practice in making decisions based on marketing research information.

SUMMARY

This case deals with the decision to open a new supermarket. Goodbuy supermarket in Oakdale, Michigan is contemplating this move. Market research uncovered many factors relevant to this decision. Census figures show that more than 150,000 people live near the proposed Oakdale Goodbuy store. There is a large breakdown of ethnic groups living around the proposed site. These groups include: black, Italian, Spanish, Jewish, and Polish. The average family income in the area was $13,500. This figure was slightly above the state average. Six competing supermarkets were also located in the proposed area, creating strong competition. These and many other factors are relevant to the decision.

These factors raise many questions such as: what product lines to carry, what media should be used to advertise these products, how well will Goodbuy fare in light of the competition, and how will the new outlet affect the sales volume of other Goodbuy stores in the area?

QUESTIONS

1. Should Goodbuy open the proposed store in view of the heavy competition it faced?

2. Should the ethnic composition of the area be a factor to consider in the marketing and advertising planning? If not, who not? If yes, which ethnic groups should receive the most attention in Goodbuy's planning.

3. If you were planning the character of the promotional approach to be used by the proposed Goodbuy store, should it be:

CASE ANALYSIS

1. Should Goodbuy open the proposed store in view of the heavy competition it faced?

The projected $300,000 in sales would seem prima facie evidence that the store should be opened but this big volume would be meaningless if substantial sales were siphoned from other Goodbuy stores in the area, and if no chance existed for these stores to make up such lost sales.

---

[1]. From Philip Ward Burton and D. Sandhusen, Cases in Advertising. Copyright c John Wiley & Sons, Reprinted with permission.

In examining the estimated losses for each of the existing stores, if the proposed store were to open, we find that by taking the middle amount for each store (as, for example, $7,500 for Harpur Village Goodbuy) we will lose $31,500 per week for the three stores. Subtracting this from the estimated sales revenue of $300,000 weekly for the new store, the volume would be reduced to $268,500. Despite this reduction, the volume would be competitive with Oakdale A & P, the current leading store in the area.

Moreover, there would be overall a dollar gain by the Goodbuy organization in the population area even if the other Goodbuy outlets did not make up their losses in the future. There is a chance that some or all of them would not make up the losses in view of the stationary population of the area for the past 5 years. Thus, recouping the losses would be possible only by taking sales directly from competing stores. These establishments would be depended upon, however, to match the increased efforts of the Goodbuy stores. Despite the assurance of the researchers that the losses could be made up through "aggressive promotional programs" the possibility of replacing the lost sales would be much brighter if there were an ascending population curve in the market area. Since there is not, it can only be hoped that the existing stores will not suffer continued losses from their present volumes.

Still, because of the projected overall gain, the risk seems reasonable. It would be a much greater risk, of course, were other big, aggressive stores to enter the area. If this happened, the older Goodbuy stores might suffer additional and, potentially serious, losses.

2. Should the ethnic composition of the area be a factor to consider in the marketing and advertising planning? If not, who not? If yes, which ethnic groups should receive the most attention in Goodbuy's planning.

With ethnic customers making up at least 61 percent of the area populations, the Goodbuy management should stock items appealing to the dominant ethnic groups and should call attention to the items in advertising. As for the degree of ethnic emphasis, the Italians, Blacks and Jewish groups should receive major attention. Least important (at the moment anyway) is the Spanish-descent group that has the lowest average income, coupled with the fact that most of the group lives in the less desirable 4 to 8 minute zone.

3. If you were planning the character of the promotional approach to be used by the proposed Goodbuy store, should it be:

   (a) Highly competitive in prices or middle of the road?
   (b) Concentrated simply on offering low prices or should it draw, as well on sales promotion techniques such as coupons, games, trading stamps, coupons, cents-off deals, and the like?
   (c) Slanted toward ethnic groups or should the marketing area be treated as a homogeneous entity?
   (d) Dignified and reflective of a quality image, or should it be unsubtle and concerned with price more than quality?

   (a) The promotion should be highly competitive price-wise. All three groups are thrifty shoppers and extremely price-conscious.

(b) The more deals the better. The ethnic groups named are constantly on the lookout for bargains with most of the shoppers checking newspapers item by item to see what dollar-stretching incentives are offered in addition to a basic low price.

(c) The advertising should not single out ethnic groups by name but by stressing in advertisements those items especially appealing to each ethnic group. Often these carry the ethnic identification such as Hebrew National Griddle Franks, or Polska Kielbasa.

(d) Dignity gives way here to hard-hitting promotion. The quality look cannot compete in the situation with the "bargain" look. Busy, hustling advertisements featuring big, black prices (low prices) and many items will win out over "clean" refined advertisements. Big areas of unoccupied white space are inappropriate. Just as crowded windows in highly promotional stores tempt a certain class of customer by offering a wide choice at low prices so do busy advertisements offer the same twin appeals.

ADDITIONAL NOTE

When the Oakdale Goodbuy store opened on a sunny April day, the mix of products and facilities it offered, as well as its advertising and sales promotion campaign designed to attract customers to these products and facilities, strongly reflected the findings and recommendations of the researchers.

To appeal to the Italian trade, for example, the following specials were announced in a pre-opening circular, distributed in Italian neighborhoods that comprised 47 percent of the population of the store's 4-minute market:

> Ronzoni Spaghetti Sauce: Buy two, get one free.
> Caruso Blended Oil: Buy two, get one free.
> Italian veal cutlets: $2.79 a lb.
> Bracioli Italian: $1.89 a lb.

The meat and deli departments of the new Goodbuy were geared toward Blacks (fresh and smoked picnice), Jews (Kosher pullets, smoked fish, Shofar franks) and Poles (Keilbasi). The facilities and special products were presented to these, and other, ethnic groups in newspaper and circular advertising. For example, cents-off coupons were offered for "any item in the appetizer department" and "any fresh or frozen meat item."

RESULTS

Opening-day sales at the Oakdale Goodbuy totaled $76,000, with a customer count of about 6,700. From the opening Wednesday to Saturday, sales totaled $277,000, and jumped to $389,000 the following week (during which the same advertised items were offered).

Best moving items were Italian veal cutlets, club steaks, and pork products.

CHRISTIANS[1]

CASE OBJECTIVES

The objective of the case is to expose the student to the thinking process and work needed to evaluate a business investment opportunity and to carry the process to the final stage of either accepting the plans or abandoning such investment opportunity.

The case describes how a group of business students started with a class project and ended with an actual business opportunity in the restaurant business. The steps followed by these students (who started with the idea of a fish franchise that was rather expensive to that of buying a restaurant at about $60,000 cost) are explained along with limited financial information collected from various sources.

The authors found that students can easily identify with this case and it can raise their interest without much interference from the instructor.

SUMMARY

The students are faced with various alternative courses of action. They can go ahead and acquire Christians as planned or they can look for another investment. They can also elect to make a counter offer to the current owner that is less than the asked price for the business. The price could be raised if the owners would agree not to compete within a range of 100 miles for a five-year period.

The students can prepare several proforma financial statements using varying assumptions to determine the effects on earnings and cash flows. These statements can aid the students in making a good decision.

Based on the information provided in the case, Christian's restaurant is a good investment. However, due to the uncertainties involved in the case, the investment should be classified as a speculative venture. In the real situation, due to the pressure involved to make a quick decision and due to the school situation, the deal fell through and the students decided not to pursue this opportunity.

QUESTIONS

1. Is Christian's a good investment?

2. Is Christian's a good bargain in terms of return on investment, at the $57,750 asking price?

3. Is it possible to convince the owners to sell it at a lower price?

4. How can the needed funds be raised?

5. Are the expected returns worth it in terms of the risks involved?

---

[1]. This teaching note was prepared by Thomas L. Wheelen of the University of South Florida, and Moustafa H. Abdelsamad of Virginia Commonwealth University. Copyright c 1984 by Thomas L. Wheelen and Moustafa H. Abdelsamad.

6. What form of organization would be the best to use in terms of legal responsibility, in reduction in the tax burden?

7. Can the group handle unforseen circumstances?

8. Is this investment viable under the most likely events without undue optimism and wishful thinking?

9. Can the group of investors work harmoniously to manage the investment without undermining their other objectives such as school or work?

CASE ANALYSIS

Pros and Cons of the Investment

Christian's as an investment seems to be promising for the following reasons. 1) The business is profitable. b) The restaurant has a developed group of loyal customers. c) Charlottesville seems to be an expanding area with regard to income. d) If the apparently popular seafood is introduced, the business could be even more successful. e) The business seems to run itself without much need for constant monitoring. That makes the investment congruent with the objectives of the prospective owners. f) The expected return on investment seems to be adequate and immediate. g) The inexpensive food business in general seems to offer a business that is less vulnerable to economic downturns. h) The determination, persistance, energy and openmindedness of teh students would give a chance for the business to grow. i) The existence of well-established busines organization is vital.

Some of the unfavorable arguments include the following. a) If the business opportunity is so great, why would the owners be willing to sell it? b) Present owners are planning to open a new restaurant that may draw customers from Christian's. c) The asked price for Christian's far exceeds the net assets which results in payment for goodwill. This goodwill is hard to measure and may disappear shortly after the old owners leave. Additionally, the goodwill figure could not be depreciated for tax purposes and would deprive the owners of the additional depreciation asociated with paying the extra costs for depreciable assets. d) The students lack the experience in the restaurant business. This inexperience may prove to be a handicap. e) Absentee ownership in a restaurant business is viewed by many to be a guarantee for failure. f) While 25% required return may seem high, it is before taxes and based on doubtful estimates. g) The students do not have their own resources. Most of the funds will be borrowed from the bank or from relatives. This would result in placing extra burdens on the new managers. Also, it will make it difficult for them to withstand any difficulties that may be encountered in the beginning. h) Dealing with employees in the restaurant business is usually a frustrating experience. It is a highly labor intensive business with much dependence on unskilled, usually less reliable (absenteeism and turnover), pool of potential employees.

Price and Return

The total investment willk be $57,750. The $500 organization expense was ignored because it can be paid from income from operations and is included in current liabilities. Additional working capital may be needed for business. Also, an allowance must be made for unforeseen circumstances.

Even though the market value of the fixed assets as listed by the CPA is $11,175, the relevant figures in buying a business are the expected earnings and cash flow. Capitalization of earnings is the right approach to use.

The sales figures for years 1, 2, 3, 4 and 5 can be adjusted as follows to estimate related cash flows.

	Years of Operation (000's)				
	1	2	3	4	5
Sales	240.0	264.0	272.0	272.0	272.0
Variable Expenses 68%	163.2	179.5	185.0	185.0	185.0
Operating Margin (32%)	76.8	84.5	87.0	87.0	87.0
Fixed Expenses (see Exh. 8)	42.0	40.9	40.9	42.4	42.4
Earnings before interest & taxes	34.8	43.7	46.1	44.6	44.6
Interest	6.0*	5.1*	4.1*	2.9*	1.6*
Earnings before bonus & taxes	28.8	38.6	42.0	41.7	43.0
Bonus 10%	2.9	3.9	4.2	4.2	4.3
Taxable Earnings	25.9	34.7	37.8	37.5	38.7
Add Back Depreciation	4.4	4.4	4.4	4.4	4.4
Add Back Interest	30.3	39.1	42.2	41.9	43.1
	6.0	5.1	4.1	2.9	1.6
Est. Cash flows ignoring loan	36.3	44.2	46.3	44.8	44.7
Loan Service	-12.0	-12.0	-12.0	-12.0	-12.0
Salvage					+20.0
Revised Cash Flows	$24.3	$32.2	$34.3	$32.8	$52.7

*Interest is based on the following amortization schedule, for a $40,250 loan at 15% annual interest rate with five year life and five annual payments at the end of each year.

End of Year	Remaining Loan	Annual Payment	Interest	Reduction Principle
0	40,250	0	0	0
1	34,281	12,007	6,038	5,969
2	27,416	12,007	5,142	6,865
3	19,521	12,007	4,112	7,895
4	10,442	12,007	2,928	9,079
5	1*	12,007	1,566	10,441

*Error is due to rounding

The internal rate of return for this investment project based on the cash flows listed above can be computed two ways.

1. The IRR based on an investment of $57,750 and the estimated cash flows ignoring the loan is 66%. The $57,750 investment covers both the loan and the students' own investment, so to compare this investment to its related cash flows, we add back depreciation and interest.

2. The IRR based on the $17,500 equity investment in the business and the revised cash flows is 158%. The $17,500 equity investment does not include the $40,250 bank loan, so the annual loan payment was subtracted in order to compare the equity investment to its related cash flows. The IRR computed on the equity investment shows the effect of financial leverage.

(A calculator was used to compute the IRR. Manual calculations may result in a slightly different answer.)

It seems from a quick examination that the price is very reasonable. The sales estimates used assume a 10% increase in Year 2 over Year 1, 3% increase in Year 3 over Year 2, and no increase in Years 4 and 5. These estimates are very conservative. Care must be taken in studying the cash flow estimates to insure that the net cash flows reflect all cash outflows. There is a tendency to underestimate costs and overestimate benefits. Comparisons can be made between Christian's experience and cost ratios in similar restaurants as found in various services such as local businesses, associations or Robert Morris Associates or Dun & Bradstreet Key Business Ratios. This comparison may reveal areas where costs are underestimated and revenues are over estimated.

Another way of looking at the situation is to ask the following question: If it costs approximately $58,000 to acquire the business, if the minimum required return before taxes is 25%, and if the business could be sold at various prices, what is the minimum annual cash flow required to satisfy these conditions? The answers, depending upon salvage value are:

Salvage Value Before Taxes	Minimum Annual Cash Flows that Would Yield 25%
$ 0	$21,567
10,000	20,349
15,000	19,739
20,000	19,130
25,000	18,521
30,000	17,912
35,000	17,302
40,000	16,693
45,000	16,084
50,000	15,475

(A calculator was used to compute these figures. Manual calculations may result in slightly different figures.)

Can the Price be Reduced

The price for any business depends upon the circumstances surrounding the transaction and the bargaining skills of the involved parties. An evaluation should be made of the likelihood that present owners could settle for a lesser price.

Financing by Owners

To reduce the dependency on bank credit and to get the present owners interested in future success of the business, the students should explore the possibility of asking present owners to receive part of their payment on cash basis and the other as a loan payable with interest comparable to the bank rate and as a percentage of future earnings. However, tying the new business closely to old owners is not advisable in the management area since it reduces the chances of implementing innovative ideas.

The students should also satisfy themselves that they have explored enough financing sources to get the best loan possible with regard to interest rate, loan life, and other terms. Contrary to public opinion, it pays to shop around for loans.

Harmony Among the New Investors

The investors should study themselves and take a hard look at their interests and personalities. Needed work and areas of responsibility must be divided in advance. Partners in small corporations are similar to partners in a partnership. They must be able to get along and agree on direction and approach to managing the business. Agreements should be made in writing and details should be stated as much as possible prior to entering into such a joint venture. What would happen if a partner wants to get his money back? How will differences in philosophy be resolved? Who will decide on general management, marketing, operations, and financing issues? Also, how much distribution of income will be expected and how will failure or success and growth be handled?

Time Element

The students were asked to make up their minds within ten days because other individuals were interested in the business. Accordingly, the analysis must be quiet yet complete as possible.

Forecasts

The provided figures are fundamental to the analysis. Therefore, a careful examination of the underlying estimates is needed. Do the cost estimates include all elements of costs and do they allow for inflation? Are sales estimates reasonable? What is the effect of future competition on these estimates? Are menu prices competitive? What is the effect of the increasingly popular fast food business on Christian's price structure and cost factors? Are fixed assets in good condition? What additional investments are needed in this area?

Other factors that could affect the success of the business include the reaction of the current employees to the change in management. Also the cook is a key individual in the success of a restaurant. What are the chances that the cook would like the present changes? Would the cook be willing to accept new changes in the menu?

With regard to the new manager to be hired, how can management insure his interest and attention to the business? How would old employees react to the new manager? How would the customers react to the new manager?

What about thefts in restaurants and lack of internal controls? Would the new manager be able to handle the situation?

Variable Versus Fixed Costs

Fixed expenses amount to about $42,000. With variable expenses of 68%, the contribution margin is 32%. Accordingly, a minimum sales level needed to cover fixed costs is about $131,250 (42,000/0.32). This amounts to average monthly sales (ignoring the seasonal nature) of about $11,000.

Concluding Remarks

The students are faced with various alternative courses of action. They can go ahead and acquire Christian's as planned or they can forget about this opportunity and look for another investment. They can also elect to make a counter offer to the current owner that is less than the asked price for the business. Conversely, the price could be raised if the owners would be willing to sign a no competition agreement within a range of 100 miles for a five-year period.

Several proforma financial statements could be prepared using varying assumptions to determine the effect on earnings and cash flows. This would help in making a better decision.

Based on the information provided above, Christian's restaurant business is a good investment. However, due to the lack of sufficient historical data, the uncertainties involved in the restaurant business with regard to competition and volume of business and due to the rather vague notion why the owners are willing to sell such a great business, the investment should be classified as a speculative venture.

In the real situation, due to the pressure involved to make a quick decision and due to the school situation, the deal fell through and the students decided to let this opportunity pass by.

Useful References

The discounted cash flow method may be used to determine the net present value of future estimates of cash flows or the implied internal rate of return under various assumptions (for a simple explanation of these techniques, see M.H. Abdelsamad, A Guide to Capital Expenditure Analysis, New York: American Management Associations, 1973).

Moustafa H. Abdelsamad, Alexander T. Kindling, and Thomas L. Wheelen, "What to look for Before Investing in Small Companies," Management Review, November, 1977, pp. 26-29, 37-38.

152

MAYTAG COMPANY[1]

CASE OBJECTIVES

This case presents the student with the problem of assessing marketing strategy in light of recent market developments. The assumption is that Maytag will continue its premium price, premium quality strategy.

SUMMARY

The Maytag Company has successfully pursued a policy of premium quality, premium price. Maytag maintains a 15 percent market share in the home laundry equipment market despite the assertion that competitive quality is now equal. The market is considered mature, but there is a possibility of a strong replacement cycle for machines installed in the 1960's growth period.

The market position of Maytag is unclear in commercial laundromats which can be described as a mature replacement market. Maytag has not been able to penetrate the home dishwasher market with a premium strategy. A private label producer and the two largest competitors control over 80 percent of the market. In the "cooking market" the assumption is that replacement and renovation will provide growth. Maytag has a strong distribution, but no national arrangements.

QUESTIONS

1. Describe Maytag's marketing strategy for its home-laundry equipment. Why has it been so successful?

2. What strategy should Maytag use for its dishwashers, considering the widely held view that Kitchen Aid is already the premium product in this product line?

3. Do recent acquisitions yield any synergy? Explain.

CASE ANALYSIS

1. Describe Maytag's marketing strategy for its home-laundry equipment. Why has it been so successful?

    Premium price/premium quality. Successful due to focus of households on the laundry, as well as to distribution and service channels. This laundry focus is probably changing; other appliances, interests, change in life styles.

2. What strategy should Maytag use for its dishwashers, considering the widely held view that Kitchen Aid is already the premium product in this product line?

---

[1].This teaching note is based on materials prepared by Lester Neidell.

This is sure to provoke controversy. My experience is that most students will want to continue premium strategy, perhaps slightly underpricing Kitchen Aid. One of the key issues here is who is the decision-maker about dishwashers. Students often miss the fact that the initial installation of a dishwasher is primarily the province of the builder. What does he look for? How big is the original installation market for dishwashers? There is a different purchaser in the replacement market. How strong are competitors in these segments? The key is that Maytag's 4-6% share of total dishwasher market may represent 25% or more of the replacement segment, and almost no penetration of the original installation segment.

3.   Do the recent acquisitions yield any synergy. Explain.

There doesn't seem to be a strong relationship between the laundry equipment and the acquisitions. The acquisitions as a group yield synergy, especially when combined with the existing dishwasher line.

This synergy is based on the kitchen. It is now possible to go to a home builder and provide a complete appliance line for the kitchen. In terms of the apartment and condominium market, Maytag is able to provide almost all appliance needs.

DONALDSON COMPANY, INC.[1]

CASE OBJECTIVES

A major focus of this case is the problem of coordinating worldwide selling and customer service efforts within the Original Equipment Group (OEG). Large customers, constituting fewer than 10 percent of OEG's accounts, are a particular problem. As their factories and purchasing departments spread throughout the world, it is imperative that `O`E`G alter its customer service methods to fit changing needs. With more than 90 percent of OEG's sales to these large customers, it is extremely important that OEG serve them properly.

Students may approach this case one of two ways. First, they may critique the planning process--its goals, procedures, selection of participants, duration, etc. While the planning process was certainly not perfect, the main goal of the case is for students to choose the most appropriate organizational structure for OEG to best serve its customers. To do this, the student must choose one of the two organizational structures presented for OEG. Students' recommendations for a preferred organizational plan should be written from Thomas Baden's perspective as vice president of OEG.

SUMMARY

Donaldson Company International (DCI) is one of the world's largest manufacturers of heavy-duty filtration equipment. While enjoying considerable past success, it experienced major losses in 1983, resulting from increasing competition and changing market conditions. These changes caused DCI to reassess its basic organizational structure, marketing strategies and corporate goals. Urgency existed throughout the organization to restore DCI's performance to previous levels.

The company broadly defined its mission as to design, manufacture, and sale of proprietary products which separate something unwanted from something wanted. The company's product line included air cleaners, air filters, mufflers, and other filtration and pollution equipment.

Both external and internal causes explained the decline of each market. Because of external causes DCI management felt that market opportunities would not rebound. To minimize the effects of the decline in worldwide trade, attention was placed on internal problems.

QUESTIONS

1. How will customers react to both plans?

2. Which plan comes closest to solving the problems OEG faced in 1983?

3. Other than the alternatives presented, what organizational structures

---

[1].This teaching note is based on materials prepared by Shannon Shipp.

exist to accomplish the same goals?

4.   Analyze the major strengths and weaknesses of each alternative. What conclusions can be drawn from the analysis?

5.   Assuming the new organizational structure is selected, how should it be implemented?

CASE ANALYSIS

1.   How will customers react to both plans?

There are three customer classifications: large, mid-sized and small. Only the large and small customers will experience a difference in the service if OEG adopts the new organizational structure.

Large customers--These firms should receive better service under the new system. Under the old system, the customer had to make separate calls for customer service, engineering assistance and ordering. With a single global account manager responsible for all communication between OEG and a customer, the customer should be able to make only one call to the account manager to place an order, request engineering assistance or secure other customer services while the account manager may in turn call on others in OEG to perform those functions; the customer need make only one call.

It does seem unusual that no formal study was conducted of large customers' needs before such a sweeping change in selling methods was suggested. OEG did not study large customers' needs formally because of time pressure to return the company to previous performance levels and the familiarity they felt with customers' needs. Students may suggest that OEG conduct a test of global account management on a few customers before it is adopted for all large OEG.

Small customers should also prefer the new plan. They will receive more frequent contacts from OEG, and be better informed about product innovations. They will also have a channel to provide OEG feedback about the level of service received and the need for new products, services and the like.

Mid-sized customers are not addressed in detail in either of the plans. This is dangerous, as these firms may be the large customers of the future. Failure to consider their needs explicitly now may lead to future strained customer relations. At the least, OEG should study their needs in more detail.

2.   Which plan comes closest to solving the problems OEG faced in 1983?

Many of the problems in 1983 were external, i.e. the simultaneous decline of major markets, strong dollar and increased offshore production and purchasing. Changing OEG's organizational structure will probably have little effect on those problems. Internal problems, however, such as the inability to coordinate customer service to multinationals and being difficult to buy from can be affected by changes in OEG's organizational structure.

OEG's inability to coordinate service to large customers is occurring where those customers have large purchasing or production facilities overseas. One symptom of the problem is DCI offices are competing among themselves for the same customers, to the detriment of DCI performance overall.

At least two reasons account for the competition among offices. First, the lack of a uniform pricing structure enables customers to shop around for the best price. Establishing a uniform pricing structure, however, might be a cure worse than the original disease. Restricting individual offices' ability to change prices in response to local market conditions would put them at a competitive disadvantage vis-a-vis local suppliers. The second problem is offices reporting to different divisions serve the same customer in different geographic locations. In North America, all offices handling mobile equipment filtration needs report to OEG, while offices handling the same product lines overseas report to International. The same customer (Caterpillar, for example) is served by OEG in North America and International overseas. No formal communication occurs across divisions so that OEG and International sometimes pursue different pricing strategies with the same customers for the same products.

Both problems, not readily soluable under the market-based organizational structure, can be addressed by adopting the proposed structure. Since all sales to a given customer, regardless of location of the purchasing facility, would be coordinated under a single account manager, price rivalry between offices would be eliminated. A formal communication link between OEG and International would also be established, allowing upper management in both divisions to clearly view how their largest customers were being served worldwide.

3. Other than the alternatives presented, what organizational structures exist to accomplish the same goals?

The case mentions three reasons why Baden should hesitate to change the two alternatives as stated.

1) The strategic development process ensured that all OEG executives had the same information on which to suggest changes in OEG's organizational structure.

2) Executives who developed the new organizational structure were responsible for implementing it. Baden could not change the plan too much without possibly losing those executives' commitment to making the new plan work.

3) The urgency surrounding the decision made it impractical to consider developing a new structure from scratch.

Without questioning the validity of these reasons, three issues seem to demand more thought before restricting all subsequent analysis to the two stated organizational structures. First, the concerns of mid-sized customers were not specifically addressed under either alternative. It is not clear if the current structure is meeting their needs. The new structure makes few changes in the current method by which these customers are served. As a result, previous mistakes in serving mid-sized customers are continued whether or not the new structure is adopted.

Second, it is questionable whether enough unbiased information was collected to choose and/or determine the most appropriate structure. Most information-gathering was done in-house by individuals with a vested interest in the outcome. For example, customer needs were identified through salesperson reports. When salespeople collect marketing research information, customers may try to respond as they think the salesperson desires, rather than as they truly feel. Conversely, salespeople may color their reports of customers' responses. Students may argue that the company should use outsiders to reduce biases in analyzing customers and competitors. Additional information-gathering by unbiased researchers may yield unsuspected customer wants which require further structural changes.

Third, a convincing rationale for changing the organizational structure has not necessarily been presented. While performance did decline from 1982 to 1983, many of the reasons were beyond OEG's control. In 1984, when those external factors began to favor OEG, it began to return to previous performance levels. Management is faced with a difficult decision--to adopt the new structure in anticipation of another downturn in external conditions, or to continue operating with the current structure and hope that the conditions of 1982 to 1983 were a fluke. In any case, the urgency surrounding the necessity for change might be misplaced.

4.   Analyze the major strengths and weaknesses of each alternative. What conclusions can be drawn from the analysis?

Current (Market-Based) Structure

Strengths
   -tried and true
   -can assess broad market trends
   -fits with organizational structure in other divisions (e.g. engineering)

Weaknesses
   -some customers straddle markets, making it difficult to assign revenues and expenses from customers to the appropriate market
   -is difficult to coordinate engineering support for those customers

Proposed Structure

Strengths
   -customer service to large customers will be improved
   -communication between International and OEG will be improved
   -small customers will receive more attention

Weaknesses
   -the global account will have many account managers reporting to him or her, which would cause management problems
   -field salespeople will have multiple bosses, creating potential for conflicting orders
   -with focus on individual customers, might lose market-wide perspective on issues affecting industry as a whole

By analyzing the strengths and weaknesses above, the following tentative conclusions can be drawn.

1) support for current strategy seems based on benefits it provides to DCI, not to customers

2) market definitions under the current structure do not reflect those used by customers

3) proposed strategy improves customer service to large and small customers, while not affecting that currently offered mid-sized customers

4) primary weaknesses of the new method are internal management issues, such as span of control, unity of command, etc.

5. Assuming the new organizational structure is selected, how should it be implemented?

There are many correct answers to this question. Rather than providing a specific implementation plan, some general guidelines for evaluating the plans are stated.

1) The plan should account for the effects the new structure will have on several parties, including the board of directors, stockholders, investment community, customers, employees, and the like. Each of these groups will be affected differently by the new plan, and must be notified of the change in such a way that DCI's image is retained or enhanced.

2) The plan should explain how the new structure will be "sold" to the group of OEG executives who wanted to retain the old structure.

3) Timing of the change should be discussed. In planning for this change, it is imperative that customers not be surprised and no gaps in service occur. Further, employees who are to implement the plan must be apprised of their responsibilities under the new plan as soon as possible to allow them to study their new assignment.

4) The plan should discuss how new communication patterns between OEG and International will be structured.

5) Evaluating salespeople under the new strategy should be discussed. Under the old strategy, directors were evaluated on the profitability of their market. Under the new strategy, directors' compensation should be tied to their accounts.

6) Some means of evaluating the new strategy's effectiveness should be discussed. Benchmarks to evaluate its effectiveness, such as improved customer relations and increased sales, should be identified.

TENNESSEE PEWTER COMPANY[1]

CASE OBJECTIVES

This case involves a new company that is trying to enter a mature market with a fairly undifferentiated product. Their attempts so far to sell pewter tableware and decorative items have not met with much success. The student must develop a marketing program on a very limited budget for this very small company.

SUMMARY

Tennessee Pewter Company, started with an economic development loan from the government, has been in business about a year. After purchasing equipment and tools from New England firms, the production line was established and began to turn out a variety of items. In the first eight months total sales volume has been $33,100 or $4,000 a month. Management feels that sales have to be at least twice the present rate to reach the desired goal of $100,000 a year.

The scope of the product line for Tennessee Pewter is comparable to competition. The only noticeable difference to the consumer may be in the fact that Tennessee Pewter products are buffed to give a polished appearance.

Independent sales reps are the traditional marketing channel. They contact department stores, jewelry stores, and gift stores. Commissions are figured at 15 percent of sales. Only two of the present customers handle a complete line of pewter from Tennessee Pewter.

Carl Dunn, the owner-operator, has solicited sales reps by phone. As a consequence, market coverage is spotty. No advertising has been undertaken principally because of lack of funds. The promotional literature sent to the sales reps consists of pictures of selected items and the names and numbers of all the items produced by Tennessee Pewter. There have been problems in filling orders and as a result a large number of back orders exist. The failure to provide quick delivery has already cost them several large orders.

Prices for the various items have been arrived at by selectively reducing competitor prices on the same item. The standard markup for the retailer is 50 percent.

In an effort to improve their operation a consultant was hired through the offices of The Center for Industrial Services in the state. Some of the general observations about the market were:

1. No brand recognition for Tennessee Pewter;
2. Size of units is too small in many cases;
3. While there is interest in pewter, buyers generally have very little knowledge of the product, and
4. Tennessee Pewter has priced its products too low in a quality market.

---

[1].This teaching note is based on materials prepared by H. Robert Dodge.

QUESTIONS

1. Where would you start in making changes at Tennessee Pewter?

2. How would you go about establishing a competitive differential for Tennessee Pewter?

3. Do you feel the use of pewter in special promotions (savings and loan premium) is a potential market for Tennessee Pewter?

4. Evaluate the future for Tennessee Pewter. Six months, 12 months, two years.

CASE ANALYSIS

1. Where would you start in making changes at Tennessee Pewter?

The obvious starting point is making the necessary changes to get orders filled promptly and shipped to customers. Tennessee Pewter can not lose orders because of poor production management. The next change should be in the product line. Sizes should be changed where indicated, the number of products reduced, and prices upped to competitive levels.

2. How would you go about establishing a competitive differential for Tennessee Pewter?

Stamping of a number on the bottom of every item much as the old touch marks would give each product individuality. Each piece would be packaged in its own box which would also include a history of pewter and a form to fill out for registering the item with Tennessee Pewter. The people's names obtained in this fashion would be a good mailing list for direct solicitation.

3. Do you feel the use of pewter in special promotions (savings and loan premium) is a potential market for Tennessee Pewter?

The premium market is ideally suited for Tennessee Pewter. In fact, the touch marks could bear the company's name or logo. Another possibility is corporate gifts.

4. Evaluate the future for Tennessee Pewter. Six months, 12 months, two years.

The next six months would seem to be a crucial time for Tennessee Pewter. Their cash flow, although no figures are given, has to be bad. They lack funds to make changes. Production may be called upon to work overtime or the work force expanded. If they survive the next six months, they should begin to grow. Desperately needed is more funding and adequate sales representation. They should probably try direct contact of nearby stores in Memphis, Little Rock, Jackson, Nashville, and Birmingham. The future looks brighter the longer they are in business, so in two years the company should start generating a modest profit.

CAMVAC, INC.[1]

CASE OBJECTIVES

This case illustrates the process one company goes through in buying out another company. The student is put in the position of having to evaluate a company as a possible candidate for acquisition.

SUMMARY

CAMVAC has grown by acquiring small companies who have technologically superior products, but are having problems in financing, manufacturing, and/or marketing. The present candidate for acquisition is a firm making oil reclamation equipment. The name of the company is Reclaim Corporation.

CAMVAC has four requirements for acquisition. One is sales volume which is measured in terms of a potential contribution of 10 percent of CAMVAC's total sales or at the present time about $10 million. The second requirement is a profit before taxes of 15 to 20 percent except in those cases where large infusions of developmental capital are needed. Sales growth, the third requirement, is a compounded growth rate of 20 percent or a doubling of sales volume every four years. Finally the product must have a strong competitive edge. In this regard the acquired firm must have the capacity to make technological modifications over a period of five years after acquisition.

The report of the project team sent to investigate Reclaim can be summarized as follows:

1. The potential market for reclaiming oil is outstanding.

2. There are two markets for Reclaim products - the add-on market where the product is sold to a firm who in turn do the job themselves and the market composed of oil reclamation service companies who specialize in this service.

3. Sales to reach $10 million would mean 2,000 Reclaim 10 models or 400 Reclaim 100 models. Sales in any one year have never been greater than 50 for either model.

4. Sales of the truck unit (Reclaim 2000) have been almost nonexistent principally because of price resistance.

5. Potentially profitable but requiring an infusion of capital is the development of an oil reclamation service division.

6. Reclaim does not have adequate manufacturing facilities. Additional capital appropriations in the amount of $4 million will be needed. The work force must be increased by 50 percent and new plant facilities are needed.

---

[1].This teaching note is based on materials prepared by H. Robert Dodge.

162

7.   Cost-of-goods-sold equals about 60 percent of sales.

8.   Reclaim is labor intensive with a non-union work force. The changeover to CAMVAC would mean unionization and an eventual increase to greater automation to offset the increase in labor costs.

9.   No company has more than one percent of the market. The real competition for Reclaim comes from disposing of oil (often illegal) in other ways.

QUESTIONS

1.   Evaluate the criteria used by CAMVAC in looking over a potential candidate for acquisition.

2.   Is the fact that Everett Manley wants to sell out and retire a plus or a minus to acquisition of Reclaim Corporation? Defend your answer.

3.   Develop a break-even analysis for the oil reclamation service division.

4.   Is the inadequacy of present manufacturing facilities a drawback necessarily?

CASE ANALYSIS

1.   Evaluate the criteria used by CAMVAC in looking over a potential candidate for acquisition.

     The criteria seem unduly harsh. A company with sales of $10 million earning 20 percent before taxes with a strong product in a growth market and no need for technological assistance is obviously ideal. However, the question must be raised as to the reason for this company becoming part of CAMVAC. Also, the price might be very steep for the company. Supposing earnings of $2 million and an earnings ratio of 10 because of the firm's growth capabilities. This would result in an asking price for the firm of around $20 million which would discount future profitability to a great extent for the buyer.

2.   Is the fact that Everett Manley wants to sell out and retire a plus or a minus to acquisition of Reclaim Corporation? Defend your answer.

     It is a plus from the standpoint that CAMVAC would not acquire the company under any other circumstances. Given the requirements for acquisition, an owner who didn't want to retire might not want to sell a company with a good potential. Rather he would seek outside funding to do what he has to do to make the firm competitive.

     From a negative standpoint, without his presence there is seemingly no one to keep the product competitive from a technological standpoint. One of the requirements concerns technological competitiveness for five years.

3.   Develop a break-even analysis for the oil reclamation services division.

Fixed Costs

Truck expenses (truck, insurance, license and fees, maintenance)	$18,750
Operation of truck (travel expenses, driver and helper salaries)	48,750
Reclaimer Service	32,000
Total	$99,500

Variable Costs

Driver 5 cents/gal. - first 100,000 gallons
    7 1/2 cents/gal. - over 100,000 gallons
Helper 2 cents/gal

Breakeven Analysis

Total revenue (200,000 gallons @ $1.25) $250,000

Less:

Fixed costs	$99,500	
Driver bonuses	12,500	
Helper bonuses	2,000	114,000
Profit for year		$136,000

Breakeven point:

Price/gal.	$1.2500
Variable cost/gal.	.0625
Contribution	1,0875

$$\frac{99,500}{1.0875} = \text{over } 91,500 \text{ gals. or } 450 \text{ gals./work day}$$

4. Is the inadequacy of present manufacturing facilities a drawback necessarily?

Yes it is a definite drawback. The reasons are: (1) labor-intensive cost that will go up with unionization; (2) need to expand labor force by a half; (3) need for capital equipment; and (4) need for new facilities.

GENERAL MOTORS CORPORATION[1]

CASE OBJECTIVES

This case presents the student with a description of an export marketing strategy. The focus in the case is on the differences between a global strategy and a more segmented, country by country, approach.

SUMMARY

General Motors Corporation has never held a dominant market position in Europe. In fact it is currently ranked sixth in the European market behind Ford, Renault, Fiat, Volkswagon, and Peugeot. In 1982, General Motors launched a campaign to become a leading European automobile producer. Its plan was to increase its market share from 9 percent to 15 percent by 1988.

At the center of the expansion program was the "Corsa," the first of General Motors' world cars. The "Corsa" was designed and initially introduced outside the United States and was General Motors' first entry in the European subcompact market. Management at General Motors thought the best market for the "Corsa" would be in southern Europe where subcompacts have a 40 percent share of the total automobile market.

General Motors reorganized that export operations are based on a free flow of components and the development of cooperative ventures. Long an advocate of free trade, General Motors has had little to say about local content regulations.

Ford as well as European automobile manufacturers fear the economic power of General Motors. Already Ford has countered General Motors' marketing push with price discounting to keep Sierra number one in the European markets. Another advantage seen for General Motors is its ability to identify the optimum level of output for each constituent part, and to make souring and output decisions for vehicles and components on a global scale.

QUESTIONS

1. What is the objective of General Motors Corporation in Europe?

2. What differences are there in the international strategies of General Motors Corporation and Ford?

3. Up to this time General Motors Corporation has been a proponent of free trade. Should this continue?

CASE ANALYSIS

---

[1]This teaching note is based on materials prepared by H. Landis Gabel.

1.   What is the objective of General Motors Corporation in Europe?

     The objective of General Motors is to be number one in Europe within a
period of 10 years. General Motors management sees one trading world. Using
the world car concept, a free international flow of components, and joint
ventures to ensure low cost, General Motors will control world markets from
one central location.

2.   What differences are there in the international strategies of General
     Motors Corporation and Ford?

     General Motors' strategy is an offensive, free trade strategy while Ford
has adopted a defensive protectionist strategy. General Motors sees one
trading world while Ford sees three. General Motors' strategy is clearly
harmed by LCR's. Ford has become interested in LCR's to counter the Japanese
threat. General Motors has actively initiated joint ventures (especially with
the Japanese and the South Koreans) to ensure lower costs. Ford visualizes
automobile producers in these countries, particularly Japan, as competitors
rather than possible partners.

3.   Up to this time General Motors Corporation has been a proponent of free
     trade. Should this continue?

     In terms of trade policy, GM and Ford are quite different. GM sees one
trading world while Ford sees three. GM's strategy is clearly harmed by LCR's
which is all the more reason why Ford should want them. But interestingly,
Ford doesn't see GM coming. All its attention is drawn to the Japanese. It
is to counter the Japanese threat that Ford has become interested in LCR's.

     GM's strategy seems to be to keep its mouth shut about European LCR's.
There is no evidence that GM is politically active. It would naturally profit
if LCR's were applied to Nissan, but it may reasonably fear that it might be
next. Question: Should GM be more proactive in defending free trade? The
company is more vocal in U.S. policy circles than in European.

     If there were to be LCR's in the EEC, how badly would GM be hurt? Its
global souring policy relies on free flow of parts, yet GM's Ascona, Cavalier,
and Kadett models exported to EFTA countries with a 60% LCR (counting the EEC
within the definition of "local") have European engines and gearboxes rather
than the more standard Japanese gearboxes and Australian engines. Thus, GM
can get under the LCR. GM could probably manage to adapt reasonably
successfully to an EEC LCR.

CAPREE MANUFACTURING, INC.[1]

CASE OBJECTIVES

This case presents a situation that allows the student to analyze the competitive position of a company. Emphasis in the case is on the utilization of sales analysis.

SUMMARY

Capree Manufacturing, Inc., after a very success-filled existence now finds itself in somewhat of a depressed market with rapidly falling sales and profits. The drop in sales from 1980 to 1981 was nearly 40 percent while profits dropped about the same relative amount. Prospects are that profits and sales will continue to taper off.

Spending to improve design of products has not brought immediate results. Small design houses appear to dominate the market with modern, up-to-date designs, usually better fabrics, and lower prices to retailers.

A sales analysis was conducted by an outside firm by the name of Driscoll and Perkins. The results show that Capree is relying on a limited part of the line to keep sales up and a limited number of effective sales reps.

QUESTIONS

1. How would you describe the market position of Capree?

2. What changes would you implement in the product line?

3. What changes would you implement in securing better sales representation?

4. If you were Donald F. Cannon, Jr., what would be your long-term strategy for Capree?

CASE ANALYSIS

1. How would you describe the market position of Capree?

Capree is in a very precarious market position. Five products account for about one-third of their sales. In contrast, their five worst performers do only four percent of total sales. The five best sales reps are six to 11 times better in terms of sales production than their poorest counterparts. Interestingly enough the top five sales reps rely upon the five best products in selling to retailers in a given territory. Unfortunately the top sales reps seem to rely extensively on a few key accounts whose purchases have varied drastically.

---

[1].This teaching note is based on materials prepared by H. Robert Dodge.

Sales coverage is deficient in several major markets. Also there is no control of sales efforts in relation to potential.

2. What changes would you implement in the product line?

Fundamentally the product line needs to be pared down. For starters, Cannon should drop the 10 poorest sellers. However since some of these products are purchased there might not be much savings in associated costs. Ideally Capree might want to keep only those products that have sales of $100,000 or more in either or both 1980 or 1981. Included in this group would be: (1) music boxes and pillows; (2) rattles; (3) shoes, books, and cups; (4) gift sets; (5) bumpers; (6) comforters; (7) crib sheets; (8) stackers; (9) zip-a-quilts; (10 safenaps; (11) carrier covers; (12) dressing bags, (13) diaper bags; (14) lamps; and (15) dust ruffles.

By cutting out almost half of the products (15 out of 29) sales are reduced only 31.3%. In addition although it is not included in the case, Cannon should reduce the range of materials and design where appropriate. New designs should be integrated everywhere possible.

3. What changes would you implement in securing better sales representation?

The first thing should be implementation of sales control based perhaps on average company sales per unit of population. In this way, Cannon and his headquarters staff could spot the weak spots in sales coverage. Secondly, poor performers should be replaced by new sales reps. This presents a problem in that the poor performers may be the best available in a particular sales territory. There might be some value in talking to the better sales reps in in an effort to expand their efforts into territories where Capree has experienced difficulties.

Still another possibility is for Capree to handle some accounts directly. Calls could be made periodically but the major share of business would be handled with an 800 number. This would require an inside salesperson, but the savings in commissions should more than offset the salary and associated costs of such a person.

4. If you were Donald F. Cannon, Jr., what would be your long-term strategy for Capree?

Sell off the production part of the company. It probably would be worthwhile to guarantee them a certain volume of business for a term of years.

Reorganize Capree as a sales organization. It might be expedient to retain several of the larger sales reps. Retire the sales manager and fire the controller. Convince Mrs. Cannon to retire from the company. Make use of Cannon and two other salespeople (hired perhaps from sales rep organizations) to call on major accounts. All other accounts could be handled with an 800 number.

Reach agreement with a design house to supply new product designs on a commission basis.

GERVAIS-DANONE[1]

CASE OBJECTIVES

This case illustrates the problems involved in fighting for market share in a maturing industry. The different marketing mix instruments must be assessed to determine impact as well as suitability for gaining a lasting competitive advantage. Impact is measured in terms of industry demand, market share, and profitability.

SUMMARY

The maturing German pudding-with-topping market is dominated by four national brands which together account for about 70% of the market. The remaining 30% are shared by about 30 regional and local competitors ("others").

Gervais-Danone, the market leader, is losing share to Dr. Oetker, a 1977 entrant, and to the "others," both of which compete mainly on the basis of price. Initially, the leader tried to protect its market share through line extensions and advertising. But as Gervais-Danone's share continued to drop, it lowered its price, first by intensifying promotional activity, then by reducing list prices. Competitors followed and the result was a general reduction in prices over an 18-month period for the entire market.

During 1982, Gervais-Danone stepped up its advertising spending and modified its products. Competitive advertising spending also increased. At the end of 1982, market shares were similar to what they had been two and a half years earlier. But prices were lower and advertising spending higher with the increase in total market demand insufficient to maintain profitability at previous levels.

QUESTIONS

1. What has happened to prices and advertising spending since 1980? What are the reasons for this change?

2. What is the impact of the different marketing-mix instruments on market share?

3. What has been the impact of the competitive dynamics since 1980 on market shares and industry profitability?

4. How will the different competitors behave during 1983, and what does this mean for market shares, industry growth, and profitability?

CASE ANALYSIS

---

[1].This teaching note is based on materials prepared by Reinhard Angelmar.

1. What has happened to prices and advertising spending since 1980? What are the reasons for the change?

    Prices and advertising spending since 1980

	1980	1981	1982
Avg retail price (DM)	0.68	0.65	0.64
Industry adv (Mio DM)	6,1	3,8	8,0
Industry demand (1000 t)	60	67	68
Adv/ton (DM)	102	57	118

    1981: strong price reduction; Gervais-Danone and Elite tried to maintain profitability by reducing advertising spending.

    1982: slight price reduction; strong increase in advertising spending by Gervais-Danone and Oetker.

    1982 vs 1980: industry prices are down; advertising spending is up.

    What are the reasons for the change?

    A. Competitors' objectives:

Gervais-Danone:	hold share
Oetker:	increase share
Elite, Chambourcy:	hold share
Others:	increase share

    Conclude: these objectives are mutually inconsistent. They must lead to a fight.

    B. Why fight on price and advertising spending?

    product: possibilities for line extensions exhausted? Everybody except Gervais-Danone pursues a me-too strategy; no significant taste differences between Gervais-Danone and Oetker (chocolate flavored products; until May 1982).

    image/positioning: no difference between blind test and as-marketed-test preferences; possible explanations: 1. advertising efforts "neutralize" each other; and 2. ineffective advertising.

    distribution: Gervais-Danone, Elite, and "others" have wide distribution--difficult to go further; Oetker and Chambourcy fight for shelf space and made price concessions.

    Conclude: lack of significant product and image differentiation focuses competition on price and advertising spending.

2. What is the impact of the different marketing-mix instruments on market share?

A. Product

Gervais-Danone modified its products in May 1982. Blind taste test results show a 80:20 preference ratio in favor of Gervais-Danone in comparison with Oetker.

- Does the taste differential have an impact on market share? Not really

- What kind of impact should one observe? Abrupt vs gradual, increase in market share, etc.

- What impact should the product modification have in order to be worthwhile?

Break-even analysis of product modification

	BEFORE	AFTER		
		No Price Change	Price Premium	Partial Price Premium
Retail Price	0.65	0.65	0.70	0.67
Net price (64% of retail)	0.416	0.416	0.446	0.43
Variable Cost	0.25	0.28	0.28	0.28
Gross Margin	0.166	0.136	0.166	0.15
Market Share	33%	40%	33%	37%

Pricing options after the modification:

- No price change: market share increase in order to maintain total gross margin: 0.166/0.136 = 1.22 x 33% MS = 40% MS

- Price premium: increase retail price by 5 pfennigs without losing market share

- Partial price premium: market share increase: 0.166/0.15 = 11.11 x 33% MS = 37% MS

Judged by the criterion of constant gross margin, the product improvement has not yet paid off: in October/November 1982, market share has only reached 35%, and there is no change in the price premium relative to competitors in comparison to the period before the product change.

B. Price
It is useful to put the 18 bi-monthly data into the computer so as to be able to call them up during the class and display various plots and regressions on a screen.

An example of a data file set up for Gervais-Danone and Dr. Oetker is shown in Exhibit 1.

Possible analyses of the price - market share relationship:

Independent Variables	Comment
price	no control for competitors' prices no control for other mix variables
price/average price (1)	controls for competitors' prices no control for other mix variables
price/average price adv/industry adv	what about distribution and the product?

(1) calculated by weighting each competitor's price by his market share

Illustrative correlations, against market share, for Gervais-Danone and Oetker:

Independent variable	Correlation coefficient
Gervais-Danone price avg price	-0.59
Oetker price/avg price	-0.55

Conclude: market shares for both firms are significantly influenced by price.

C.   Advertising

The same kinds of analyses as suggested for price can be performed.

Independent variable	Correlation coefficient
Gervais-Danone adv/industry adv	0.07
log (Oetker adv/industry adv)	0.76

Conclude:

- Gervais-Danone's advertising does not appear to have an effect on its market share. Why? Price and advertising efforts confounded (but multivariate regression produces non-significant advertising coefficient - see below)? Ineffective advertising copy (compare also blind test vs as-marketed test results).

  Nonetheless, Gervais-Danone's advertising raises the stakes for the other firms. For example, Oetker's share of voice would be higher (and, maybe, its market share) if Gervais-Danone spent less on advertising.

- Oetker's market share seems to be strongly affected by its advertising share.

Illustrative multivariate market share models (n=18)

Dep V. <u>intercept relative price relative adv</u>   <u>R-2</u> <u>DW</u>

MAGD   PGDPI   AGDAI   .35 1.26
          186.92   -146.34   -0.17
          (t=3.47)   (t=2.8)   (t=0.9)

MAOE   POPI   L(AOAI)   .69 2.05
          27.25   - 14.10   0.17
          (t=4.54)   (t=2.4)   (t=4.3)

                                        (DW = Durbin-Watson)

<u>Conclude</u>: relative price is significant for both firms; share of
voice is significant only for Oetker.

D.   <u>Distribution</u>

<u>Distribution and market share</u>

The distribution penetration of Gervais-Danone, Elite, and the
others remained more or less unchanged between 1980 and 1982.

Oetker improved its distribution by 6 points during 1982, yet its
market share remained stable. Chambourcy's distribution increased
by 10% during 1981 and its market share went up by 3%. Thus,
although an increased distribution penetration generally means a
higher market share, there appears to be a great deal of
variability.

<u>Distribution position of each brand</u>

Dividing market share by distribution penetration provides an
indicator of each brand's distribution position:

	Market Share divided by Distribution Penetration				
	GD	OE	EL	CH	Others
1978	56	10	11	35	29
1979	49	11	12	29	31
1980	40	18	11	22	37
1981	39	18	11	21	36
1982	38	17	12	20	35

<u>Gervais-Danone</u>: Although its distribution position has been
declining, it still remains the number 1 brand for the retailers who
carry it, and the dominant national brand.

<u>Oetker</u>: 1980 was a particularly good year for Oetker: it gained 7
points in distribution and at the same time strengthened its
position with each retailer. But since then, the brand has been
stagnating in the number 4 position, far behind Gervais-Danone.

Elite: Elite has a wide distribution thanks to the effective Unilever sales force, but its number 5 position in the trade indicates its vulnerability.

Chambourcy: Initially (1978) in a strong number 2 position, Chambourcy's wider distribution has resulted in a loss of depth.

Others: The local and regional brands occupy now a very strong number 2 position behind Gervais-Danone.

It is of interest to note that the dairy products specialists - Gervais-Danone, Others, Chambourcy - have a stronger distribution position than Oetker and Elite, who have no specialized sales force.

3. What has been the impact of the competitive dynamics since 1980 on market shares and industry profitability?

A. Impact on Market Shares

Between 1978 and 1980, market shares changed considerably. But since 1980, the annual market shares have remained pretty stable, even if bimonthly market shares still vary quite a bit.

What are the reasons for the market share stability since 1890?

B. Change in Gervais-Danone's Objectives and Behavior

Before 1980, market shares changed mainly at the expense of Gervais-Donone, who used line extensions as a main tool and tried to maintain price levels. Since then, Gervais-Danone has been fighting in order to hold its share, even if it means lowering its price.

What accounts for this change?

- Change in market growth: Before 1980, the strong market growth compensated for the market share decline. Since 1890, market share maintenance is necessary to hold and/or slightly increase volume. Market stagnation creates a double zero-sum game: for market share, and for volume.

Industry Growth and Gervais-Danone's Sales Growth

	Ind-Sales (1000 t)	T/T-1	GD-MS	GD-Sales (1000 t)	T/T-1
1978	42	?	48.4	20.5	?
1979	52	24%	43.2	22.5	+10%
1980	60	15%	35.5	21.3	- 5%
1981	67	12%	34.0	22.8	+ 7%
1982	68	2%	33.9	23.1	+ 1%

- Change in Gervais-Danone's product portfolio: initially, Dany+Sahne "accounted for the bulk of Gervais-Danone's sales and profits." The company may have needed the profits from Dany+Sahne in order to launch new products that would reduce its dependence on one product. In 1981, Dany+Sahne accounted for 24%, and in 1982 for 21% of sales. It is conceivable that other products are now highly profitable; but this is unlikely - the case indicates a 1982 profitability of 0.3% in 1981 (1.1/326) and 0.6 (2/362) in 1982.

Share of Dany+Sahne in Gervais-Danone's Total Sales

	1981	1982
Sales (1000 t)	22.8	23.1
Nr of 125g cups/kg	8	8
Cups (Million)	182.4	184.8
Retail price/cup (DM)	0.66	0.65
Dany+Sahne retail sales (Mio DM)	120.4	120.1
Dany+Sahne net sales (64%)	77.5	76.9
Gervais-Danone total sales	326	362
% for Dany+Sahne	24	21

- Changing trade-offs between market share and profitability: Gervais-Danone knew it could not maintain its initial 100% share. Its objectives probably were: to maintain a certain "minimal" market share, and to ensure high industry profitability. Their behavior suggests that the aimed-for "minimal" market share must have been around 40%. When share declined significantly below 40%, GD decided to sacrifice profits in order to maintain share.

C. Failure, on the part of all competitors, to build a lasting competitive advantage

Price was the main weapon used by the followers to take market share away from the leader. The major reason for using price in this market is the speed and strength with which price affects market share. But price had the following drawbacks in this market:

- rapid imitation by competitors was possible: trade promotion activities and list prices could be modified very rapidly if necessary; in fact, Exhibit 9 indicates a strong correlation between competitors' retail price movements.

- prevailing profitability levels made a price-war likely: profit levels in 1980 offered sufficient leeway for a price war. Competitors who responded to price cuts with a lag and, therefore, had to offer an even greater price cut in order to get back their previous market share, were able to do so. To maintain their share advantage, the initiators cut price even further, etc.

- the competitors who used price had no decisive cost advantage:

according to the case, only the "others" had a lower production cost (DM 0.24) (but also a lower quality) than Gervais-Danone (DM 0-25 before the product modification). Excluding the possibility of cross-subsidization, GD is the only national brand that would have survived a really serious price war.

Conclude: no one was willing to give up market shares; no one was able to keep temporary market share increases.

D.   Impact of competitive dynamics on industry profitability

1981 vs 1980

price change:	-4.5%
advertising change:	-38.22%
demand change:	+11.7%
industry price elasticity:	11.7/4.5=-2.6
industry advertising elasticity:	11.7/38.2=-.31

These bi-variate elasticities are difficult to interpret, because price and advertising changed at the same time. Possible biases:

- observed price elasticity is too low: without the reduction in advertising, industry demand might have increased even more.

- observed negative advertising elasticity is spurious: without the price reduction, industry demand might have declined.

Sales:	+ 7% (observed price elasticity is 1)
Contribution I:	slight decline
	necessary demand increase would have been: (0.44-0.26)/(0.42--.26) = .18/.16=+12.5
	implied industry price elasticity: 12.5/4.5=2.78 (vs 2.6)
	major reason for the high necessary price elasticity are the constant production costs
Contribution II:	increase in absolute amount, due to cut in advertising spending
	slight decline (36% vs 37%) as a % of sales

<u>1982 vs 1981</u>

price change:	-1.5%
advertising change:	+110.5%
demand change:	+1.5%

industry price
elasticity: 1.5/1.5=1

industry advertising
elasticity: 1.5/110.5=0.0136

possible biases in elasticities:

- price elasticity too high: without the advertising increase, demand might not have increased at all.

- advertising elasticity too high: without the price decrease,
  demand might not have increased at all.

Possible explanations for the lack of demand responsiveness to price
and advertising during 1982:

- change in price too small to be noticed by consumers.

- other factors reduced demand: e.g., economic slowdown during
1982.

Sales:	constant (price elasticity = -1)
Contribution I:	strong decline because of price reduction and production cost increase
	necessary demand increase would have been: (.16/.14) - +14.3% half for the price reduction; the other half for the production cost increase
Contribution II:	strong decline both in absolute terms and as % of sales

<u>Conclude</u>: Evolution since 1980.

- output:	+13.3%
- sales:	+ 6.7%
- marketing contribution (cont. II):	-13.0%

Competitive action has not changed market shares much, but has
reduced industry profitability.

<u>Average industry price, industry advertising,
and industry demand</u>

The 18 bi-monthly observations can be analyzed in order to see what influences, if any, the average price and total industry advertising have on industry demand.

Illustrative results are as follows.

Indept var	Correlation	Regression Coeff't	t
intercept		226.498	7.277
avg price	-.811	-228.589	-5.341
log (ind'y adv)	.173	1.096	0.625

R-2 = .67
Durbin-Watson - 2.05

Conclude: industry demand is sensitive to price, but not to advertising. Advertising, at best, serves to shift market shares.

4. How will the different competitors behave during 1983, and what does this mean for market shares, industry growth, and profitability?

A. Competitive behavior during 1983

Competitors' behavior during 1983 will depend mainly on:

- assessment of industry attractiveness (size, growth, profitability, etc.)

- assessment of the relative competitive strength

- strategic importance, to each competitor, of the pudding-with-topping market

B. Industry attractiveness

Size:

- 68,000 tons vs 348,000 tons for the entire pudding market: 20% volume share

- prices are about twice as high as for traditional pudding: ca. 40% value share

- 1982 net sales are DM 348 million

Volume growth:

Arguments in favor of low growth:

- consistent reduction in growth since 1978

- no great possibilities for product line extensions

- 60% penetration already high

Arguments in favor of medium to high growth (i.e., between 5 and 20%):

- 1982 was special because of economic slowdown; economic recovery will stimulate market growth

- 60% penetration is low relative to yoghurt (75%)

- possibilities for line extension not exhausted (package sizes - low consumption by households with four or more children; types of packages - e.g., nicer packages for festive dining; etc.)

- price reduction will stimulate growth: particularly low consumption among: farmers, households with 4 or more children, low-income consumers

Profitability:

Arguments in favor of poor profitability prospects

- apparently low barriers to entry for local and regional dairy companies: raw product availability; no need to advertise; pudding-with-topping completes existing product line; short distribution channels

- local and regional competitors are low-cost producers who, in addition, may not have the same profitability objectives as the national brands

- presence of different types of competitors makes coordination difficult; multinational branded dairy products companies (Gervais-Danone, Chambourcy, Elite) vs dessert company (Oetker) vs cooperative (most "others") vs family-owned company (e.g., Ehrmann)

- too many national brands given the many line extensions per brand (many different flavors) and the limited shelf space. Oetker and Chambourcy will attempt to gain a distribution coverage similar to Gervais-Danone and Chambourcy, is, obtain between 15 and 19 more distribution points. To succeed, they will have to make price concessions.

- incompatible market share objectives

- slow-down in market growth creates incompatible volume objectives

- competition focuses on price

- advertising does not stimulate industry growth: possibility of an advertising war that leaves everyone poorer off

- limited possibility to escape price competition via product differentiation: imitation is easy; consumer choice on basis of price rather than quality (see Gervais-Danone's experience with its product modification)

- only 1/3 of customers are brand-loyal

Arguments in favor of good profitability prospects:

- price has stabilized during latter half of 1982: the industry has learned its lesson

- advertising copy is poor: possibility for product differentiation via better advertising

- product differentiation via packaging

- only 17% of consumers buy systematically the least expensive brand

C. <u>Relative competitive strength of major competitors, and strategic importance of pudding-with-topping market to them</u>

The financial consequences of different strategic options for 1983 for each competitor, can be analyzed using an electronic spreadsheet set up like the data in Exhibit 2.

GERVAIS-DANONE

<u>Strengths</u>

- dominant market share
- broad distribution
- number one brand with distributors
- dairy products leader; board line; specialist image
- specialized sales force
- superior product
- most profitable of national brands
- part of diversified company: possibility for cross-subsidization, if necessary

<u>Weaknesses</u>

- ineffective advertising (poor copy?)
- production cost (after modification) significantly above "others"
  - vulnerability in case of a real price war
- very low company profitability

<u>Strategic importance of pudding-with-topping market</u>

- 21% of total sales
- probably very important for profitability
- own production

<u>Conclude</u>: market is very important to Gervais-Danone

<u>Likely objective for 1983</u>: hold market share, no matter what

<u>Marketing mix</u>: avoid price competition (especially after the
product modification); look for synergy between superior
product and advertising: improve advertising copy; search for
product line extensions (packaging, etc.)

Dr. OETKER

<u>Strengths</u>

- relatively low sales force costs
- effective advertising
- probably high brand awareness of Dr. Oetker (assumption)
- image of dessert specialist (assumption)
- diversified company: cross-subsidization possible

<u>Weaknesses</u>

- number 3 national brand with stagnating market share
    - inferior product (10/80)
    - no own production
    - no specialized sales force
    - limited distribution
    - weak position with distributors
    - narrow dairy product line: pudding-with-topping = 88% of
      Oetker's dairy products sales
    - limitative marketing behavior; emphasis on price
    - low profitability relative to market leader

<u>Strategic importance of pudding-with-topping market</u>

- only growth segment in the pudding market, with 40% of value of
pudding market
- about 2% of Oetker's packaged foods sales

<u>Conclude</u>: the market is important for a dessert producer, but
Oetker has entered late, and its commitment is weak (no own
production and sales force).

<u>Likely objective for 1983</u>: Oetker has three options

- increase market share: this requires considerable commitment and
  resources, as the market leader has shown that he intends to maintain his share

- hold market share: perpetuate the status quo of the last six
months. This is an uncomfortable situation, but it may provide
  a "bridgehead" for future expansion of Oetker's dairy products
  line

- milk: let market share decline by reducing advertising spending
  and increasing price

Marketing mix: varies depending on the market share objective.

CONSEQUENCES OF COMPETITIVE SCENARIOS: MARKET SHARES, INDUSTRY GROWTH, AND PROFITABILITY

Three scenarios are:

1. Competitive warfare

   This scenario will take place if

   - at least one of the competitors seeks a major market share increase: e.g., Gervais-Danone, Oetker, or the "others"

   - none of the other competitors is willing to yield market share

   One may speculate about the chances of a "shake-out." Who would be most likely to yield in case of war?

   Oetker: low commitment; low profitability

   Elite: own production, but no specialized sales force; average profitability; pudding-with-topping is 17% of Elite's sales

   Chambourcy: high commitment; high stakes (pudding-with-topping is 30% of Chambourcy's sales); but low profitability

   Others: low-cost producers

   Conclude: Oetker seems most vulnerable

   If price is the major competitive weapon, this scenario is likely to stimulate significant market growth.

2. Status quo

   This scenario will take place if no one has strong market share ambitions, yet no one is willing to initiate a price increase.

3. Cooperation to increase industry profitability

   Here, market shares stay pretty much as they are. In addition, someone initiates a price increase, and the others follow.

   This appears possible as far as the national brands are concerned. The big question mark are the "others."

   This scenario is likely to lead to market stagnation.

THE DENVER ART MUSEUM

CASE OBJECTIVES

The purpose of this case is to consider a not-for-profit organization's marketing mix and, in particular, the role its pricing strategy, has on accomplishing its organizational mission.

SUMMARY

The Denver Art Museum is the official art institution for Denver. In 1971 it was relocated into a new six story building. The museum's permanent collection consisted of 35 thousand objects with the largest single portion being American Indian art. Twenty special circulating exhibitions were shown at the museum each year.

The museum had a number of educational programs including lectures, tours, films, seminars, dance, mine, music and other performing arts. The museum attendance averaged over one-half million per year. The museum was closed on Mondays and open 40 hours per week, including one evening. The Denver museum had traditionally been free to the public. However admission fees had been charged for major circulating exhibits. The museum director asked: "In the new building we had a double budget, a new board of trustees, quadruple attendance and a challenging question: how can we best use this building?"

The museum relied heavily on private funding especially a museum associates program. In 1982, the total allocation of funds from the state of Colorado and the city and county of Denver was reduced by about 25 percent. In addition, federal funds were slated for a 50 percent cut. Due to the budget cuts the museum was considering the implementation of a "recommended" admission fee.

QUESTIONS

1. Briefly describe the product, distribution, promotion, and pricing aspects of the Denver art museum's marketing mix.

2. From a marketing point of view what is the Denver art museum's organizational mission?

3. Does the new pricing strategy conflict with the Denver Art Museum's marketing mix or organizational mission.

CASE ANALYSIS

1. Briefly describe the product, distribution, promotion, and pricing aspects
   of the Denver Art Museum's marketing mix.

   The product offered by the museum in its broadest sense is education and
entertainment. The specific permanent collection and the temporary
exhibits provide a more specific definition of the product.
          Since the museum is in a permanent location its distribution is
similar to the situation of a retail store.

   The case provides limited information concerning the promotional strategy
of the Denver Art Museum. However one might assume that publicity and direct
mailing are their major sources. The pricing situation points out that the
Denver Art Museum has many publics. The museum associates program indicates
that a large contribution fee is exchanged for a feeling of civic pride. This
civic pride is an intangible aspect of the total product that is exchanged for
a "price." Thus price and product take a broader perspective in this sense.

2. What is the Denver Art museum's organizational mission?

   The Denver Art Museum briefly defines its mission as an educational
mission. However, there are entertainment aspects to the museum's art
collection and its performing arts programs. Thus, from a consumer's
perspective the consumer may choose to visit the Denver Art Museum rather than
attending a movie or a Denver Bronco football game.

   The mission statement might be expanded to say to provide an educational
opportunity to all segments of the population. Hence, the museum's efforts to
attract lower-income visitors might receive special emphasis, if this is the
case.

3. Does the new pricing strategy conflict with the Denver Art Museum'
marketing mix strategy or its orgazational mission?

   The student should be encouraged to think of the various prices the
museum offers to various target markets. The admissions fee is a specific
price, perhaps exchanged for a days "entertainment," to the general public.
The optional fee aspect of this fee allows the museum to reach its mission of
attracting lower income visitors. However, low income visitors might feel
like "second citizens" if they are observed not contributing. That is, as
others walk in paying they may feel conspicuous and think others may see them
as "sneaking in." However, the voluntary nature of the plan does allow low
income and young visitor's the opportunity to visit rather than to avoid the
museum. One alternative to an optional payment strategy is to have a day free
well publicized for everyone. Thus, a low income visitor can visit the museum
on a "Tuesday." The pricing strategy also may reduce peak periods such as
Saturday traffic. There are pro's and con's to both options and these can be
raised in class.

The key to setting prices is to achieve certain price objectives. Maximizing visitors may not achieve maximum profit. Many museums have various classes of membership and hence prices. For example a system of prices with associated benefits (product) might look as follows:

MEMBERSHIP

Regular

*Invitations to exhibition previews and special events
*10% discount in Museum Shops
*Monthly Calendar
*Free admission to exhibits with fees

STUDENT AND SENIOR CITIZENS

Same as above but lower membership fee.

SUSTAINING

all General privileges, plus
*Reciprocal membership in participating museums
*Special preview invitations

PATRON

all preceding privileges, plus
*Invitations to distinguished lectures series
*Listing in annual report
*Meetings with visiting artists and experts
*Out of town exhibitions and collections

This may allow for multiple pricing objectives to be achieved.

DEEP SOUTH CIVIC CENTER[1]

CASE OBJECTIVES

The purpose of this case is to elvauate the corporate mission and marketing strategy and tactics for a not-for-profit organization.

SUMMARY

Lafayette, Louisiana, is a city of approximately 90,000 people located in the Arcadian section of Louisiana. Arcadiana comprises most of the southwestern section of Louisiana ranging from Baton Rouge on the east to Lake Charles on the west. Most of the area is rural.

The economy of the area is based on sugarcane, cotton, and rice farming; the fishing and seafood industries; and oil exploration. Also many oil companies engage in exploration and production activities along the Louisiana coast and offshore in the Gulf of Mexico.

In the late 1950s Lafayette's only public gathering facility, the Lafayette Municipal Auditorium, caught fire and burned to the ground. At that time Lafayette was experiencing increasing decay in its downtown area. Some slum areas had developed and the general quality of life in the city suffered from a lack of cultural activity.

The burning of the old auditorium sparked some of the city fathers to begin thinking about what was happening to their downtown area.

Shortly after the fire, discussions began in the Lafayette City Council regarding the future of downtown and of Lafayette.

Discussion also centered around what appeared to be a growing trend in convention and trade show activities throughout the South. The city fathers felt that the central location of Lafayette, between New Orleans and Houston, would provide opportunities for regional and statewide conventions and trade shows. They hoped this would help promote the overall economy of the city and bring economic benefits to the retail businesses, motels, and restaurants. They discussed the need for facilities that could be used for social events such as weddings and banquets, as well as the need for a sports arena for the local high school basketball games, gymnastics events, and the like.

The City Council decided to construct the civic center. George Smith was hired to manage the Deep South Civic Center. George had been in the amusement management business. George felt that to be successful in his new position he had to improve the image of the civic center in the community. He also felt the "profits" needed to be high. "The big money is in booking concerts in our coliseum," according to George Smith. "If we want to maintain a bottom line that won't cause the City Council to get into an uproar we've got to make sure we book enough concerts during the year to generate the revenue we need...

---

[1] These teaching notes based on materials prepared by Dr. Jeffrey D. Schaffer, University of New Orleans. Used by permission.

Conventions bring a lot of people to the city but all we get is the fixed daily rate. With the labor rates we have to pay, it costs us more than we take in. The same is true for operas and symphonies because they get the fixed civic rate."

"Our plan is to try to keep everyone happy. We have to book some conventions and cultural events as well as cater to local civic groups. But we can't let them get in the way of events." George Smith said the primary reason for not engaging in more direct selling is that they don't have the four to five additional slide presentations they need as a selling tool. Their one slide presentation, entitled "Booking a Concert," has been shown frequently at local civic club meetings and at city high school presentations. The management also advertised and engaged in sales promotion activities. "Most of our business comes because we are here," said George Smith. "Our sales promotion is on a day-to-day basis... The city doesn't have enough hotel rooms for us to go after the big conventions and our airport is served by only one carrier."

QUESTIONS

1. Outline the goals of the Deep South Civic Center.

2. Outline the strengths and weaknesses of the organization from both a managerial and marketing perspective.

3. What strategic problem faces the Deep South Civic Center?

4. What are the operating problems facing the Deep South Civic Center?

5. What environmental factors influence the Deep South Civic Center?

6. What recommendations would you make to the managers of the Deep South Civic Center?

CASE ANALYSIS

1. Outline the goals of the Deep South Civic Center.

The goals of the organization

1. To attract new industry to Lafayette - especially oil related.

2. To meet competition from other cities in this regard.

3. To help reverse the decaying environment of downtown Lafayette.

4. To provide a facility that could be used to enhance the cultural and entertainment of the city (relates to A and B).

5. To provide suitable meeting space for civic groups.

6. To have a facility that would encourage trade shows and conventions to meet in Lafayette.

7. In relation to (6) to promote the overall economy of the city.

8. To provide a facility that could be used for local social events.

9. To provide a local sports arena.

10. To have a facility that would be self-supporting.

11. To provide a facility that will benefit the overall good of the city.
2. Outline the strength and weaknesses of the organization from both a managerial and marketing perspective.

Strengths of the organization.

1. Modern complete full service facility (relatively minor inadequacies).

2. The facilities should be completely paid for (financed through 15 years bonds issued in 1963).

3. Central geographic location - half way between New Orleans and Houston.

4. Located in the heart of Louisiana's industrial growth area (petroleum).

5. Experienced management in the entertainment field.

6. Experienced operations supervisor.

7. Existing sales person on staff.

Weaknesses of the organization

1. Unclear lines of authority and responsibilities within the city structure.

2. No statement or communication of organizations (city's) goals.

3. Internal reporting system almost non-existent.

4. No internal financial management.

5. No operational guidelines or standards.

6. No specific sales program.

7. Very short term outlook by management.

8. Overwhelming budgetary process.

9. Ineffective use of budgetary guidelines that are employed.

10. Inflated labor costs.

12. Lack of direct managerial control of important operating policy decisions (i.e., role of commission is misdirected).

3. What strategic problems face the Deep South Civic Center?

Major strategic problems

1. <u>No clear statement of the mission of the civic center</u>. Although it has
    been relatively easy to identify the key factors involved, these factors
    have not been documented and effectively communicated. Rather, they have
    been lost in the shuffle.
2. <u>Strategy of the organization</u> as are result of no clearly identifiable
    objectives from above <u>has been developed by the operating management</u>.
    Because of very short range evaluation techniques on the part of the
    City Council no long range criteria were ever established. The facility
    has developed a highly negative image and in order to survive, the current
    manager had to adopt a posture of appeasement to the press and local
    community coupled with attempting to maximize revenue generation
    (definitely not in keeping with implied objectives of the civic center).

3. There has been <u>no analysis of potential opportunities</u>. First with respect
    to the city as a whole, that is the integration of the civic center into
    overall objectives of the city with respect to economic development (i.e.,
    new hotels, restaurants, cultural events, city wide development of public
    areas, etc.). Secondly, with respect to the civic center itself, in terms
    of identifying other marketing opportunities. Identification of other
    opportunities must be done in light of the overall mission, objectives,
    risks and resources of the civic center.

4. <u>Board of Directors</u> (Civic Center Commission) <u>is ineffective</u> and does not
    address itself to strategic matters. First, the composition of the board
    does not bring the necessary talents to bear to support the civic center
    from a strategic standpoint. It is totally made up of lay citizens, as
    opposed to a make up of people who could bring important talents to the
    strategic process. Secondly, the board deals with operating issues that
    should be left to operating management (i.e., advertising, promotion,
    rates, ticket sales, etc.).

5. <u>A way to evaluate the performance</u> of the civic center <u>from a strategic
    standpoint</u> has not been established. Therefore, operating management has
    applied its own survival strategy (i.e., minimize the loss). A method of
    evaluation needs to be established that will measure, in relative degree
    of importance, the benefits in terms of overall contributions to city wide
    economic development (conventions and trade shows), cultural benefits,
    civic meeting benefits, etc.

6. <u>Effective communication of mission and goals</u> of the civic center to the
    city wide population has never taken place. This must be done so as to
    eliminate the type of negative image created in the past.

Minor strategic problems

1. Lack of an overall marketing strategy incorporating, overall mission,
    goals and objectives, comprehending the opportunities, risks and resources
    and outlining key market objectives and how they are to be achieved. This
    would comprehend the degree to which the facility was to be used for

conventions and trade shows, cultural activity, sports activities, civic meetings and events, etc. It would establish sales, promotional and public relations methods and techniques and provide for the use of appropriate media resources.

2. The need for the development of an appropriate information system in order to communicate strategic goals and objectives and monitor feedback internal and external to the civic center.

Presently, executives are not applying any of the strategic management components of analysis, formulation, implementation, interpretation and evaluation to the management of the civic center. The strategies being utilized are those that have been developed intuitively by the civic center manager. It appears that these strategies have been developed in response to the lack of strategic goals communicated from the city and a very short sighted evaluation approach used by the City Council.

The current management perceives its survival and continued success based on its ability to appease the local community, maintain a low public profile, avoid negative publicity and to generate enough revenue so as to maintain operating losses at current levels or less.

4. What are the operating problems facing the Deep South Civic Center?

Major operating problems

1. Lack of an integrated marketing plan.

2. Lack of an effective management information system and appropriate management reports.

3. Lack of internal financial/controllership personnel.

4. Need for operating standards regarding utilization of labor.

5. Need for streamline of the budgetary process and effective integration of that process with a meaningful management information system.

Minor operating problems

1. Inability to utilize less expensive part-time labor.

2. Need for greater control of the arrangement between civic center and catering/concession contractor.

5. What environmental factors influence the organization?

External

1. The local media and its propensity to exploit a negative situation.

2. The lack of sophistication within the community to appreciate and recognize benefits beyond immediate financial success.

3. The competitive situation involving other towns and cities in the area.

4. The influence of natural resources (oil primarily) relative to the growth of the area.

5. Local government policy.

Internal

1. Excessive (higher than market) labor rates set by the city Finance Department.

2. Relationship (authority over) with concessions/catering contractor.

3. Certain physical restrictions within the facility (lack of adequate small meeting spaces).

4. Parking limitations.

Resources involved

1. Debt free, modern, full service civic center.

2. Growth area.

3. Managerial talent within community - corporate executives.

4. Central location of city.

6. What recommendations would you make to the managers of the Deep South Civic Center?

Strategic recommendations

The key issue with respect to the Lafayette Civic Center is its total lack of a strategic approach to the direction, operation and evaluation of the facility. The mission and objectives of the facility are implicit in the reasons for its development, however, they have never been clearly identified or communicated to either the city as a whole or the management of the civic center. The lack of clearly communicated goals and objectives has resulted in the use of performance evaluation criteria that emphasize not only the short run but the wrong results.

Clearly, there is a need to define the mission, goals and objectives of the civic center. This has to be accomplished through a basic restructuring of the strategic management hierarchy within the city government, including redefining the roles and responsibilities of the top management from a strategic standpoint.

Alternative structures:

I. Reorganize the civic center as a separate non-profit corporation and the commission as a key strategic management entity (Board of Directors)

process and see that it is composed of people who can bring appropriate talent to bare on the strategic process. Have the civic center manager report directly to this commission.

II. Eliminate the civic center commission entirely. Place the civic center under the direct control of the City Manager who, through the City Council, will be responsible for establishing the strategic management framework for the facility.

III. Continue operating under the present framework.

These three alternatives represent important broad perspectives through which the solution to other strategic issues can be approached. The implementation and potential effect of the strategic management process will be predicted on which of these alternatives is selected.

Criteria to select an appropriate solution

The criteria to select an appropriate solution in this case needs to be viewed from two standpoints. First, and most important, will be the determination of which of the three alternative perspectives to choose. (I. e., (1) reorganize the civic center and commission; (2) eliminate the commission; or (3) continue under present framework.)

This can be done through a careful presentation and documentation of:

1. The implied objectives for the development of the civic center.

2. The historical results of the civic center to date in meeting these implied objectives.

3. The factors necessary to the strategic management process.

4. The anticipated results of effective employment of the strategic management process (i.e., more effectively meeting the objectives).

This type of analysis should show that both alternatives III and II are likely to be lacking in their ability to effectively achieve the overall objectives of the civic center. Intuitively based on the state of the civic center as it now is, alternative III (continue operating under the present framework) has not been effective in addressing and meeting the implied objectives of the civic center.

Likewise, it would seem logical that, although closely interrelated, the administration of the City of Lafayette and the management of the civic center are substantially different. It would seem highly unlikely that the management of the civic center, from both a strategic and operations standpoint, could be effectively integrated into the city administration. This factor is supported by the overwhelming budgetary process imposed by the city on the civic center, most of which is totally irrelevant to the needs of the civic center.

The second level of criteria are those which will be used to select the alternative strategies to achieving the stated objectives of the civic center. In this regard, a means of first measuring the perceived needs of the community in terms of the uses to which the civic center facility can be put is required. This can be accomplished through a series of questionnaires designed to measure the relative degree of importance of the elements of the overall mission of the civic center (i.e., how important is having conventions relative to cultural activities relative to entertainment activities, etc.)

Subsequently, an evaluation procedure can be established putting appropriate weight on the uses to which the facility can be put and possibly a scale can be developed relating overall economic benefits, cultural benefits, civic benefits, etc. This then would provide the basis for evaluating alternative strategies that can be employed relative to the opportunities that may exist for achieving the various objectives of the civic center in light of the risks and resources required and the potential benefits.

Final recommendations

1. Restructure civic center commission

    a. Define its purpose as the strategic control group for overseeing the strategic management of the civic center.

    b. Define the composition of the commission so as to provide talent resources appropriate to the needs of the civic center.

        1. The City Manager or high level planning official.

        2. Top level member of city's financial community.

        3. Top level member of city's hospitality industry (hotels, restaurants).

        4. Representative of cultural interest in the community.

        5. Representative of community's civic organizations and/or sporting interests.

        6. Top level business executive or strategic management expert from academic community.

        7. Voting member of the City Council.

        8. The manager of the civic center.

    c. The commission is to be self perpetuating, that is to have the responsibility to select its own successors within the context of maintaining the cross section of talent outlined above. Recommendations for new members are made to and approved by the City Council.

d. Each commission member is to serve a term of five years with the City Manager, City Council representative and civic center manager to be perpetual members. The five year terms are to be staggered.

2. Through the restructured commission delineate the mission of the civic center. (I.e., to serve the benefit of the overall community of Lafayette through contributions to the overall economic and cultural welfare and growth, by providing a facility to promote and support cultural development, entertainment, civic organizations, conventions, trade shows, sports events and social activities for the community.)

3. Begin to assess the relative level of strategic uses that might be appropriate for the civic center. This could possibly be accomplished as a breakdown of the number of days (or percentage of time) the overall facility was used for a particular purpose.

4. Restructure the city/civic center hierarchy to provide a more direct means of communication of the policy making/strategy development functions of the commission with the management of the civic center.

> Civic Center   City Council
> Commission
>
>
>
> Civic Center   City Manager
> Manager

5. Begin to assess the marketing opportunities in relation to determined city wide strategic usage, and the risks and resources involved.

6. Based on findings from above design a strategic marketing plan comprehending

    a. specific objectives
    b. internal talent required
    c. external resource
    d. media resources
    e. long range cost benefit relationship

7. Design and implement an internal management information and reporting system that will permit both appropriate operations and strategic factors to be evaluated.

8. Integrate the budgetary process of the civic center with the needs of the operation and with overall organizational strategies.

9. Provide for restructuring of the internal management of the civic center to permit the addition of appropriate financial management, the establishment of labor standards and effective lines of authority.

Civic Center Corporation
Commission

Civic Center
Manager

Civic Center Financial
Manager/Controller

Assistant Civic Center
Manager Operations

Promotional
Coordinator

Ticket
Sales

Accounting
and
Management
Information

Parking
Lot
Supervision

Operations
Superintendent